TURNING
P·O·I·N·T·S

by

Bill Pearce

Provocative and Meaningful
Devotional Reflections

NIGHTSOUNDS

721 East State Street, Suite 302
Rockford, Illinois 61104
(815) 987-3978

INTRODUCTION

TWENTY YEARS OF
NIGHTSOUNDS

Have your ever stopped during your busy life to say to yourself, "I wonder where I'll be... and what I'll be doing ... 20 years from now? Two decades ago, as I finished 25 years as an announcer-musician at WMBI, the flagship radio station owned by the Moody Bible Institute in Chicago, I asked myself the same question ... and ... beautifully enough, the answer is here: 1993 is our 20th anniversary year of the NIGHTSOUNDS ministries.

It's amazing to look back and see how the merciful hand of God gently led us. It was almost like running an obstacle course to begin an independent radio program, yet the Lord blessed our efforts to carry NIGHTSOUNDS around the nation and into other parts of the world through missionary radio.

Twenty years later you'd think we'd be looking only backwards to the start-up of NIGHTSOUNDS. Actually, we believe that God's work through us is far from completed. He has much more for us to do, not just in this new decade, but unto the next century. There are technical advances to allow even more people to hear Christian radio more clearly and more widely than ever before. So, we look into the future.

Our listeners often tell us that NIGHTSOUNDS reaches many more unchurched people than "traditional" Christian radio programs. Perhaps that is so. We know that when we sit in the studio, we try to sense His direction and share His message as we talk into that microphone, hoping that the selected music will capture listening hearts.

So ... NIGHTSOUNDS is God's work when it works ... and Bill Pearce's when it doesn't ... when it goes over someone's head or misses the mark.

I suppose the fact that it <u>does</u> work is the great miracle. We know, intellectually, that NIGHTSOUNDS is God's work, and it's effective. Yet it constantly amazes me. As I sit in the studio and put together the creative and spiritual components for a program that is aired some eight weeks later, only God's Holy Spirit can orchestrate the supernatural time elements so that men and women of all ages, people from all walks of life and every profession imaginable can listen at the same time, yet hear a variety of messages. They tell us that only God could have spoken to a unique need or problem that they have at that moment.

> "Not by might, nor by power,
> but by my spirit, saith the Lord of
> hosts"   (Zechariah 4:6).

MIRACLES VIA RADIO

During 1993, we'll celebrate the 20th anniversary of NIGHTSOUNDS. Five nights a week, we combine music and low-key thoughts to effectively use the medium of radio. In the quiet hours of late night, we reach out to tens of thousands of people living on the edge of eternity, of desperation, of panic, of hopelessness.

Somehow, God uses NIGHTSOUNDS to touch these people in the desperation of their need at that specific moment of time.

May I share just a brief glimpse into the lives of a few of those who have been touched by God through the ministry of NIGHTSOUNDS? Some are dramatic ... others commonplace ... but each is unique, real, and miraculous.

A letter from a young drug user read: "A friend told me to listen to you. No one else ever told me that Jesus loved me ... despite all the things in my life. An amazing thing happened: I accepted Christ as my Saviour." That woman is now off drugs ... loves and serves God ... and has married her friend.

A young assistant minister was to visit a hospitalized parishioner, one of the stalwarts of the congregation, who was dying. "I didn't really feel prepared to deal with the dear old saint", he wrote. Still, he jumped in his car at 10:30 P.M., asking

God to give him wisdom. He was amazed, "your topic 'happened' to be 'ministering to the dying'. During the 30-minute drive to the hospital, your program prepared me to face the situation with complete peace. I'm certain God planned the entire timing."

I take no personal credit for such experiences. When I go into the studio to record the broadcast, it may be morning, afternoon or late at night, depending on my schedule and God's direction. However, it's always five to eight weeks before the actual air date. So, only God in His infinite wisdom can have any idea how I can say something at 2:00 P.M. in Rockford, Illinois, that will touch the heart and mind of someone many weeks later, at night, listening in New England, the "Deep South", on the West Coast, or just about anywhere.

And only God could have directed to have a bedroom clock radio go on at 10:40 P.M. in a small Indiana town inside a house filled with despair and conflict, where a wife had decided that she could live no longer with all the pain and problems besetting her. She had devised a plan to kill her children and then take her own life.

Only God could have planned that my subject would be "Suicide," and as the clock radio unexplainably turned itself on, this woman heard me saying, "If you're in the process of taking your own life, STOP for just a moment, please. Listen to me." That halted her in her tracks. Even in her desperate state of mental frustration and confusion, she was forced to stop and think.

Then the woman somehow found a pastor in a Bible-believing Church, asked for counseling, and accepted Christ as Lord and Saviour! Our office has never been more jubilant than when we read of the final outcome.

Some write to tell us simply that NIGHTSOUNDS gives them peace as they go to sleep, or is their companion on the late shift.

Please don't ask me to explain how God can use the same program to soothe a spiritual wound for one person, while it becomes a sword to cut away the hardness of sin surrounding the heart of another.

I can't explain it, but I trust you'll join me in rejoicing that God does it ... and share the strange mixture of humility and pride I feel, knowing that God (for His own reasons) has chosen to use NIGHTSOUNDS and me in this unique ministry.

> "But the salvation of the righteous is of the Lord: He is their strength in the time of trouble."
> (Psalms 37:39)

LISTENING WITH YOUR EYES

One of the reasons I enjoy meeting personally a listener to NIGHTSOUNDS is that one-on-one exchange. It's one thing to receive a letter from someone, but what a difference to meet a person whose soul carries an expression of love, reflected through the eyes. And, I've noticed that frustration o joy can both be understood most clearly through eye contact.

Psychologist Theodore Reich said, "We are obliged to listen to one another, not just audibly, but with our eyes and with the third ear of empathy, compassion, and understanding."

After a recent concert was finished, I saw an elderly couple approaching me. I could see their intensity. The man stayed a bit behind and his wife grasped both of my hands and just looked at me with tear-filled eyes. She said nothing. She didn't need to because her eyes were speaking for her. In them, I saw joy, gratitude, tenderness, and strength. They spoke volumes.

Other eyes I've seen are empty. Some are alive and sparkling. Still others are what my mother used to call "shifty".

And at another concert, one fellow carried on an entire conversation with me, never looking at me once.

I've seen the love of Christ in certain eyes. In other eyes, bitterness and even hatred.

The Bible says Jesus looked with compassion upon the multitudes. I can also imagine His eyes flashing with indignation as He drove the money changers from the temple; or of His eyes welling up with tears of grief as He learned of the death of His friend, Lazarus.

Can you imagine what went through the mind of the apostle Peter when Jesus' eyes met his shortly after Peter denied Him? Or ... can you visualize His look of forgiveness for the woman taken in adultery?.

Jesus said in Matthew 6:22 "The eye is the lamp of the body. If your eyes are good, your whole body will be full of light" (NIV).

God has promised to guide us with His eyes (Psalms 32:8).

We're sending out signals with our eyes constantly. Have you ever been cut in half by "a look"?

A raised eyebrow across a room can either devastate a person or support him.

Have you ever looked into a little child's eyes and seen the Garden of Eden? No guile, no criminal intent, no politics, no divisiveness. "Jesus looked on the multitudes ... with compassion." God can speak ... through our eyes!

> "The eyes of the Lord search back and forth across the whole earth ... looking for people whose hearts are perfect toward Him"
> (2 Chron. 16:9).

QUIETNESS

NIGHTSOUNDS is an attempt to instill quietness and confidence into your life, late at night, after the noise bombardment of the day has taken its toll.

It's great to be part of a product that creates tranquility and quietness.

With the introduction of what we've commonly recognized as "noise pollution" into the fibre of daily living, sometimes we just give in to it and put up with it, just as we might treat a chronic backache.

In creating you and me, God designed into us a need for quietness. In fact, the qualities of justice, peace, confidence, and quietness are all linked together in Isaiah 32:17.

Noise can be a definite source of tension, whether it's the incessant barking of a dog, a noisy TV or stereo "boom box" with the volume too high, motorcycles tearing past, roaring jet planes, screaming sirens, or whatever noise pollutant offends you most. All of these discordant noises create tensions, making it more difficult to deal with the normal pressures of life.

Is there anything we can do about it?

Yes, don't shout at those around you. Turn down the volume of the record player, radio of TV. Check your auto muffler; be consciously aware of others' sensibilities and need for quietness. This is especially true in the haven of the home environment. Each of us can do a little more to bring down the decibel level in the world around us.

"Be still, and know that I am God."   (Psalms 46:10)

ARE YOU HUMBLE?

The way we answer a question like this may indicate whether we are or are not. I can almost hear certain responses:

"Well, I'll have to be honest and say ... yes!"

"Humble? Who, me?"

"I don't even know the meaning of the word."

"No, I am anything but humble. I'm egocentric!" or, "Can't you tell?"

I guess this is a difficult concept for us to talk about. But you know, Jesus made it clear that humility was a vital part of the Christian experience, central even to the process of salvation.

Many great men of the Bible displayed this virtue: Abraham, Moses, David, John the

Baptizer. Their greatness to a great extent, was based on their humility.

Bishop J. C. Ryle mentioned that only the <u>small</u> birds sing. Geese, cranes or turkeys honk or make noise, but they do not sing. Even the gorgeous peacock doesn't sing. Instead it is canaries, larks, and nightingales that fill the air with their music.

This phrase struck me when I first saw it: "The branch that bears the most fruit is bent lowest to the ground."

There is no better role model to show us what humility is like, except Christ Himself.

One man of God said: "From the time of His voluntary birth in a stable to the moment of His voluntary death in crucifixion, He was flawlessly true to His own testimony, 'I am meek and lowly in heart.'"

We ask Jesus Christ to make us humble, yet we may have to learn the hard way because this lesson is usually learned through discipline or sacrifice.

We've been told by James to "humble yourselves in the sight of the Lord" (James 4:10). Perhaps this should be an immediate personal priority!

> "Whosoever therefore shall humble himself as this little child, the same is the greatest in the kingdom of heaven"(Matt. 18:1-4).

ARE YOU ABLE TO LAUGH?

Are you kidding? What is there to laugh about any more? The nightly news broadcasts, TV reports and magazines seem to contain only the most grim news and information. But I suppose we could begin by laughing at ourselves.

Sometime ago, a manufacturer of foreign import automobiles used the "laugh at yourself" strategy in its advertising and the VW "think small" campaign quickly made the car maker #1 in the market.

God created us with the capacity to laugh, probably because He knew that we'd really need it.

I think it might have been Mark Twain who said, "Man is the only creature who can laugh at himself ... or needs to!" I fear for people who have no sense of humor. I understand Adolph Hitler was one who lacked a sense of humor.

The Old Testament character, Job, was one we ordinarily wouldn't think would have much cause to laugh. Yet, he was one in Scripture who spoke positively about laughter when he wrote: "He will yet fill your mouth with laughter ... and your lips with shouts of joy."

Laughter can come from deep within, welling up from a heart overflowing with joy. But laughter like any other good thing, can be used wrongly, as in cruel, vengeful or divisive laughter.

Let's ask God to give us the enjoyment of good wholesome laughter.

Now and then I'll hear happy laughter filtering through from one of our adjacent NIGHTSOUNDS offices and it makes me feel great. It's a good sign. People who take themselves too seriously aren't much fun.

Do you think God laughs?

Voltaire once said that God is a comedian playing to an audience that's afraid to laugh.

Well, any God who created the ostrich, monkey, or platypus had to have a sense of humor. A monk in a monastery, in the twilight of his life said: "If I had to live life over again, I'd make more mistakes. I'd relax ... limber up. I'd be sillier. I'd eat less beans ... and more ice cream."

God richly gives all for our enjoyment, and we ought to have some fun with life.

> " ... go out with joy, and be
> led forth with peace: the mountains
> and the hills shall break forth before
> you into singing, and all the trees of
> the field shall clap their hands."
> (Isaiah 55:12)

HORSE SENSE

I was reprimanded once for advising a listener in a letter that, "We, as Christians, don't need to have a Scripture verse for everything we do during the day."

While I'm glad for the Biblical guidelines that direct us along our daily paths, I'm afraid we also have too much legalistic teaching in evangelical Christianity. We add to God's direction all kinds of baggage that has nothing to do with true spirituality.

I recall hearing an account of a railroad agent somewhere in Africa who had been reprimanded for making decisions without first getting his orders from headquarters. So one day, his superior received the following startling telegram:

"Tiger on platform eating conductor.
Wire instructions."

God has certainly given most of us the gift of common sense. Sometimes it really would be a relief to hear a voice from heaven spelling out each move we make -- to the letter. But, then we'd not need to walk by faith anymore. We'd probably become "spiritual robots."

There's a balanced philosophy of living to be found in the divinely-inspired library of wisdom, God's Word. As one of the psalmists wrote: "Thy word have I hid in my heart, that I might not sin against thee" (Psalms 119:11).

Sin? Do you ever talk about it? Now wait -- don't turn the page. I realize that discussions about sin are not fun. Such times can be haunting, provoke guilt, and remind us of how short we fall of our goals. Any serious person would admit that it bothers us that we fail.

Also, we fool ourselves; "Maybe, if I don't think about sin, it just might go away!" But we should take a look at our clay feet. We need to know where we miss the mark. We need to identify the patterns.

And guess what? There's hope. We can be "cleansed of all unrighteousness." We've been given a pattern, a perfect pattern, that we as human beings can emulate. God says, "Be ye holy, as I am holy."

OUT TAKES

I recall some nights back as I was in the process of recording NIGHTSOUNDS, a strange voice came booming through my headset saying, "Okay, why don't we just unload a case of Super-Glue so they can put it all together again!"

That cryptic sentence, shouted into his CB radio by a passing trucker, was picked up by my microphone. It only took up about eighteen inches of audio tape, amounting to just some three or so seconds of time. But it was indelibly recorded as part of a NIGHTSOUNDS broadcast, and I couldn't send the program out to the hundreds of radio stations with that few second interruption as part of the tape.

I waited until program's end, and the alien sentence was spliced out. No one will ever know about it except you and me.

In the thousands of recording sessions I've been involved in, there are always the out takes. Some are very funny. Some would be quite embarrassing.

I'm thinking of two occasions now, where I was introduced to large audiences via out takes. Certain engineers had saved my little verbal mistakes and frustrated comments I had made, either on the air or in recording sessions, put these on a single tape and used it as a humorous and novel introduction.

15

Aren't you glad that God doesn't dig up all of your past "flubs" and drop them right in your lap? So many of life's "out takes" would be hard to live with, at best.

Conversely, we have God's promise in Psalm 103 that, "As far as the east is from the west, so far hath He removed our transgressions from us." We've been assured that, "He'll remember our sin no more" (Jer. 31:34).

In other words, we won't have to live with, -- or even listen to -- our "out takes!" That's worth praising Him for!

A WOMAN ALONE

A man in your life walks out on you ... your spouse has died. Maybe it's by choice, but in any case you find yourself ... a woman ... alone.

And, without sounding like a typical life insurance salesman, I'm reminded that sometimes life doesn't always prepare us for these challenges. Sure, there are lots of self-help books on getting over our grief, and plenty of radio or TV programs on surviving emotionally. But where will you live? What about expenses? What do I do about the business, or even the ordinary details that he cared for before?

Don't be afraid. I tell you with some authority that you will get through this experience. And surviving emotionally and spiritually will lead you to people who, like yourself, have been able to cope. They can help you help yourself.

These gifts of help and direction sometimes come from those who later become your friends. And you will need friends. So don't be afraid if you are a woman alone.

Dismiss your grief and decide to live again. You are not alone ... even in solitude.

"I will not leave you comfortless: I will come to you."
(John 14:18)

STRESS

The fast-moving pace of life in our modern society has produced an ugly by-product called stress. Out of the hundreds of letters that come to us each week, a third or more are what can be identified as "stress" mail.

Stress was first defined as a specific syndrome in 1935 by researcher Hans Selye. Since then it has become an urgent concern. Over a thousand published articles a year focus on stress.

Each time I open the NIGHTSOUNDS microphone, I am conscious of the fact that every one of us has some area of stress or pressure crowding us from within or without. Some of us never mention it, but keep the pressure continually suppressed.

I understand that until this century heart disease was not a major medical problem. Now, almost a million Americans die from it each year. Medical sources inform us that the stress of modern living plays a significant role in not just the onset of coronary difficulties, but in a variety of other illnesses as well.

No matter how good a Christian you are, you are not immune to the strain of living and the attendant temptations and pressures. Yet, we are made in God's image, with resources, Scriptural promises, and spiritual dynamics that work wonders.

It's from this base that we deal with the various areas of stress most often mentioned by our listeners. We draw on the counsel and expertise of ministers and specialists in the field on human behavior, working from the absolute of God's Word.

Meanwhile, let's thank God and work from this eternal keystone: "Thou wilt keep him in perfect peace whose mind is stayed on Thee, because he trusteth in Thee" (Isaiah 26:3).

Some time ago, a Catholic nun wrote to tell us that for years she had trouble sleeping at night until someone suggested listening to NIGHTSOUNDS as a remedy. Several weeks later, she wrote again to inform us that after hearing NIGHTSOUNDS, she fell into a deep sound sleep. Consequently, her physical condition improved and this was followed by a brighter emotional outlook.

Although we have received many letters similar to this one, we aren't suggesting that NIGHTSOUNDS will immediately bring therapy to your soul. However, the framework from which we work each night -- a total trust and daily yielding to God -- provides a rational structure for making momentous changes in life-style.

There is such a thing as "Spiritual Medicine." When people are shown that they are created in the image of God, it gives them dignity and purpose. Spiritual, emotional, and mental health comes as a result of a proper relationship with God, Who helps us on a daily basis to reach maximum fulfillment in all areas of life.

So, although NIGHTSOUNDS is not simply a cure-all for stress and sleepless nights it may be the beginning of a vital, new outlook for you!

"And the peace of God, which passeth all understanding, shall keep your hearts and minds through Christ Jesus." (Philippians 4:7)

WHO IS MOST IMPORTANT?

It was after a concert at Park Street Church in the city of Boston some years back. I was meeting and greeting many in the audience, when an unassuming man in a plain grey suit approached. He introduced himself, and thanked us for the performance.

As we talked, I casually asked him what type of work he did. He responded, "Oh, I sell insurance." We exchanged a few more remarks, then he politely shook my hand and was on his way. As the man walked alone out of the door, one of the church officials, came up to me.

Do you know who that man is? he asked.

I replied, "Yes ... he said he's an insurance salesman."

The church official replied, "Not just an insurance man -- he's the president of the John Hancock Life Insurance Company!" At that point all I could think of was Chicago's John Hancock Center, then the second tallest building in the world! And judging from the humility of the "insurance salesman", many must have overlooked his prestige and office.

It's been somewhat fascinating as I've had opportunity to be with presidents of colleges, universities, or large businesses. Sometimes I've commented to them something of their position or accomplishment, but invariably they almost always become a bit embarrassed or self-conscious.

The message I receive loud and clear, especially if this worker is a Christian, no job is more significant in God's eyes than another. Our social scene assigns status and power based on an individual's achievement and occupational level.

Yet, unlike society's stratifications, all jobs are equally important in God's sight. The Lord doesn't classify us by our income of professional status, for God welcomes various talents and abilities in His service.

Just look at Jesus' disciples: fishermen, doctor, tax collector, politician. What each of us can do is to surrender what we have to the Lord and allow Him to use us for His glory!

"By humility and the fear of the Lord are riches, and honor, and life." (Proverbs 22:4)

EVEN YOU ARE HUMAN

... and so am I. We are both very much aware of it. It's tough to keep discovering that we are still afflicted with many of the same patterns of temptation and sin that we had come to Christ to get rid of.

It's one thing to make an occasional blunder, but another to falter again and again in the same old pattern of failure.

Our humanity seems to manifest itself most obviously at the point of our dominant weakness.

Doubts begin to creep in. We worry about the reality of our conversion or the power of Jesus Christ to deliver on what He's promised. We think maybe we've been "oversold."

Are you plugging away, hoping or praying that some instant "magic" will take over? Listen to this:

> "Reliable is the message and deserving of wholehearted acceptance, that Christ Jesus came into the world to save sinners, of whom I am foremost. But, I found mercy so that to me, foremost, Jesus Christ might display His unlimited patience to be an example to all who shall put their trust in Him for life eternal"
>
> (I Tim. 1:15-16, Berkeley).

I used to think that Paul the apostle was presumptuous and conceited to tell us to "Follow me as I follow Christ." But, he was simply stating, for the simplest believer as well as the most intellectual theological heavyweight, that his life was an example of the unlimited patience of God.

Are we sometimes baffled by our own failures, poor conduct and sinful inconsistencies? So was Paul. But like Paul, we are to follow Christ. We pick ourselves up, confessing our failures to a God who understands our human frailty, and move forward in faith.

"So ... comfort and encourage
each other with his news"
(1 Thessalonians 4:18, LB)

NO HANDS BUT YOURS

Many years ago at the Winona Lake (Indiana) Bible Conference, I happened to overhear a conversation between two Christian leaders who were having breakfast.

The late president of Moody Bible Institute, Dr. William Culbertson, was asked by the late, beloved physician, Dr. Walter Wilson, "Have you thanked God this morning for the fluid that surrounds your eyeballs?"

Dr. Wilson's rather "far-out" question reminds me that often we take too many things for granted. Even though we don't think about them, they are essential.

In the courtyard of a quaint little church in a French village, a beautiful marble statue of Jesus stood with His hands outstretched. One day, during World War II, a bomb fell nearby and the statue was all but destroyed.

After the battle, the citizens of the village tried to reconstruct their beloved statue. Although no great masterpiece, this statue of Jesus with outstretched arms had become a cherished part of their lives. In fact, if anything, the scars of war seemed to enhance it.

But their enthusiasm soon dimmed. They could not find the hands of the statue. "It is impossible! We cannot have a Christ without hands," someone observed.

Then, another idea was offered and prevailed. Today a brass plaque points to the scarred statue with a great gospel message: "I HAVE NO HANDS BUT YOUR HANDS."

Let us thank God for giving us the opportunity and the ability to be HIS HANDS in the world today.

And, perhaps we should take a little time to think of all He has given us ... things we take for granted ... and use without thinking ... or even remembering to thank Him.

> "I have no hands, but your hands,
> to do my work today.
> I have no feet, but you feet,
> to lead men on their way.
> I have no tongue, but your tongue,
> to tell men how I died.
> I have no help, but your help,
> to bring men to God's side."
> -- Unknown

WINDOWS

Did you know that there's something called a "simulated window"?

In certain hospital rooms, where there are no windows, a simulated window, with a pretty view is placed on the wall. Behind this pleasant scene is simulated light that moves as the sun would move across the sky. It's been proven that this window does wonders, keeping patients bright and upbeat, fostering their healing process.

And when we moved our NIGHTSOUNDS studio recently, the carpenter had to cover up a window. But instead of the usual carpentry and wall coverings, a plan was made to create a view outside this otherwise useless window. A three-dimensional representation of the Chicago skyline is now an inspiring new "view" as I look out of my studio.

Windows are important to us -- they're metaphors of how we look at things. Even the eyes are considered the "window of the soul."

How are your windows? Fogged? Clear? How you look out ... and look in ... your windows is probably a good indication of how you see your life.

No wonder we are uplifted ... when our windows are clean.

"But the man who looks

intently into the perfect law that gives freedom, and continues to do this, not forgetting what he has heard, but doing it -- he will be blessed in what he does." (James 1:25, NIV)

FOR THE RECORD...

The rhythm section was already in the recording studio, tuning up in their respective booths for acoustic isolation. The audio engineer, meanwhile, was setting the sound levels for the various microphone placements, when my daughters Laurie and Shannon, and I walked into the control room. It was the beginning of another recording day at the Pinebrook Studios, Alexandria, Indiana (near Indianapolis).

John Innes, pianist for the Billy Graham Crusades, was producing our recording session, as well as playing the keyboard instruments. As we planned and discussed the format of this record album, we decided that this would be a somewhat mellow album, embracing some of the older as well as more recent Gospel songs, interspersed periodically with Scripture narration and trombone interludes.

Neither Laurie nor Shannon had ever been

in a professional recording studio, not to mention performing in one. The producer accommodated the keys of the songs to their vocal range and, after some of the "butterflies" and apprehensions were gone, we got down to business.

After Laurie's rendition of "Father's Eyes" and Shannon singing "It Won't Be Long," it was my turn. We enjoyed the privilege once again of "praising the name of God with a song," and "magnifying Him with thanksgiving" (Psalms 69:30).

Although we were performing in a studio, it was still a spiritual experience. There was no audience to play and sing to, to provide reaction to what we're doing, yet we knew that many thousands would eventually hear what we recorded.

Somehow, because God was there, we performed up to an ability He had given. This happens as sometimes He helps us perform "over Our heads."

For example, I was "just practicing" one trombone interlude. In practice it worked so well, I muttered, "I hope I can do that again when it's time to record."

But producer John Innes had already recorded it. As is sometimes the case, he had instructed the engineer to tape the rehearsal. I tried several more "takes," but none quite matched the quality and performance of the practice "take."

Another time, we were reading a Scripture passage to see if it might fit the space between the vocal sections of the song. The exact passage God led me to read, and at the specific rate He directed me to read aloud, fit to the exact word, to the very split second. Maybe we should have recorded the "hallelujahs" from the control room!

> "And thine ears shall hear a word behind thee, saying, "This is the way, walk ye in it ... "
>
> (Isaiah 30:21)

HOW IS YOUR ATTITUDE?

It kept Dr. Victor Frankel alive in a German Concentration camp.

It allowed football players like Joe Namath and Merlin Olsen to continue to excel ... long after their legs gave out.

It's what keeps widows going after their spouses pass away.

It's more important than our job, our bank account, or the way people think of us. And all it is ... is a choice.

But it's the single most important decision you or I can make today.

It's ... our choice of <u>attitudes</u>. The single idea that keeps us going or cripples our progress.

We can choose the determination to endure ... or the paralysis of defeat and self-pity.

It's your choice.

> "Finally, brothers, whatever is true, whatever is noble, whatever is honorable, whatever is right, whatever is pure, whatever is lovely, whatever is admirable -- if anything is excellent or praiseworthy -- think about such things." (Philippians 4:8, NIV)

HEADWINDS

I was on my way home from a concert hundreds of miles away and had just settled down in my seat when the "fasten seat belt" sign came on.

The pilot's voice over the intercom said, "We're facing a 65 mile-per hour headwind today. But relax, folks … we'll get there."

And, true to his word, a short time later we circled O'Hare airport only a few minutes late. We landed safely at our destination, and taxied to the gate none the worse for the buffeting headwinds.

Inside the plane we wouldn't even have noticed the gale force winds pushing back at the airliner. If the pilot hadn't told us, we'd have never known of his struggle to overcome the headwinds and maintain control of the plane and our schedule.

So, how's your day going? Are you facing terrific headwinds? Maybe it's hard to get motivated or follow through with your routine in a particularly creative way today. That's okay. Keep your eye on the goal. Pace yourself. And know that no matter what resistance you face, you will eventually reach your destination safely, because your Pilot is in control.

We can even profit when we think there is an insurmountable force that confronts us. Who knows? By staying on course, we may find that the headwind turns out to be a blessing. For you see, in aerodynamics, it's the headwind that provides the lift.

> "They that wait upon the Lord shall renew their strength; they shall mount up with wings as eagles; they shall run, and not be weary; and they shall walk, and not faint."
> (Isaiah 40:31)

WHERE DO I TURN?

There I was; driving toward my destination, directions in hand; but the streets weren't marked.

Has that ever happen to you? It's frustrating, isn't it? And yet, have you ever been in the same predicament -- no street signs -- and yet you just "knew" which street to turn down because of some intuition or inner prompting? This has happened to me and I simply thank the Lord for leading me to turn at a particular junction or He guides me to take a certain off ramp. And, "somehow" I find where I'm going.

We look for such "signs" in life. Many people say their faith would increase if Noah's Ark could be discovered ... or if the Shroud of Turin was real. Or if God would show Himself in some specific way. In our quieter moments ... it probably does not make much difference.

When we're still enough ... we probably don't need signs.

But, even then we're looking for one ... we wander through the valley of shadows and listen as best we can, yet we still hear nothing. So we're reminded: do your best and keep on keeping on. Sooner or later -- we trust -- the right direction shall appear.

"Trust in the Lord with all

thine heart; and lean not unto thine own understanding. In all thy ways acknowledge Him, and He shall direct thy paths."(Proverbs 3:5,6)

AIMING FOR THE HORIZON

In just a few short years, you and I (and the rest of the world) are facing what could be a frightening new era. But in our march toward the year 2000, we must remember that, as we strain to see hope beyond the grim world headlines, we have available to us a comprehensive and realistic overview. The Lord Jesus Christ has given us a future filled with hope.

Why can we confidently look to Jesus? Never once did He ever infer during the course of His daily speech that anything could take God by surprise, that nothing would defeat His Heavenly Father.

Never once did Jesus talk "defeat." He spoke only of "victory." At Calvary, Jesus was victorious, atoning for the sins of each one of us. Since then, He has been pleading with people to let Him give <u>them</u> the power to live victoriously.

But you hurt. And I hurt. Is this a contradiction? -- a lie? No, it's simply that we

35

haven't been promised a painless life or freedom from frustration. Jesus was frustrated, yet He never lost control. He never prayed from a position of panic. His nerves never betrayed Him. Jesus never gave a sharp or hurtful answer to those whom He loved just because He was tired.

I want to share with you what a friend shared with me, his own affirmations from his morning devotions. Just before my friend stepped out of his front door into an uncertain world he'd say, "I am loved. I am wanted. I am needed. I make a contribution to the world. I am a beautiful person, precious in God's sight, today, if frustration comes my way, I will turn toward God at once. I will not indulge in negative projections or responses. I am God's child. I will recognize Satan's suggestions and temptations and call upon the Lord to walk me through the devil's traps. JESUS IS LORD OF MY DAY!"

> "God is our refuge and strength, a very present help in trouble. Therefore will not we fear, though the earth be removed, and though the mountains be carried into the midst of the sea."
> (Psalms 46:1,2)

GO FOR IT!

You were probably watching, as I was during August, 1992, when the summer Olympics were telecast from Spain. No doubt one of life's greatest thrills would be to stand on the highest of three pedestals and bend forward to receive the Olympic gold medal for winning an athletic event. I can almost feel the hair on my neck stand up as our flag is raised and the sound of our national anthem fills the stadium, -- put yourself in that fantasy -- to be lauded as the greatest athlete in the world! This is your joyous payoff for the long hours, months, even years of training, self-sacrifice, and agonizing discipline. Now here you are -- world champion!

The challenging phrase, "Go for it!" at some point, must have challenged the gold medal winners to an all-out, continuous effort.

Yet there is another event of worth. It's the greatest contest of all -- the Christian life! We don't have to display bulging muscles, dazzling speed, or breath-taking physical coordination for this event. But it demands a great deal in terms of personal self-discipline and dedication, mixed with a healthy amount of patience, to attain God's goal for our lives. The apostle Paul uses this metaphor of the race in Philippians 3 in describing the training for living the Christian life.

If you have not read this passage from

Philippians 3 in awhile, why not take the time to do so today?

I learned the hard way many years ago at a school track meet that a distance race is NOT a sprint! It's an endurance contest that involves pacing, timing, and a "reserve" or power for the "kick" on the stretch!

My friend and fellow Gospel singer, Bev Shea, told me that he "just wants to finish the course with honor." The Apostle Paul reminds us that it's the finish of the race that is most significant -- not the flashy way we might come around the first turn.

The incorruptible crown mentioned in 1 Corinthians 9:25 could well be called the crown of faithfulness.

So, "go for it" by persevering in your own race.

> "Those who are wise ... shall shine as brightly as the sun's brilliance, and those who turn many to righteousness will glitter like stars forever" (Daniel 12:3).

ARE YOU SATISFIED?

Alexander the Great brought fear to the hearts of the early civilized world, but is said to have wept after his final conquest because there were no longer any nations to conquer.

Benito Mussolini, who, through his arrogant will, wished to see Italy restored to the grandeur of the Roman Empire. Yet, he died pathetically and his naked body was hung upside down in the streets.

The Soviet dictator, Josef Stalin, was a tyrant who was as feared and hated by his countrymen as his enemies. But in the end, he was a broken, lonely man at his death.

Adolph Hitler, was another madman who terrorized the world. He committed suicide in a bunker, his power and greatness gone in an instant.

What would have satisfied these men? More power? Wealth? No.

There's a famous rock group which has sung for over twenty-five years. Despite fame and vast wealth, they still can't get satisfaction.

Satisfaction -- that elusive state for so many -- is never attained by "things". Satisfaction is found as a state of mind.

The Word of God says, "Be anxious for nothing." And therein lies the truth. Satisfaction can only be gained through peace within.

GOD'S GREAT DISAPPOINTMENT

No purposeful person wants to leave an important project unfinished. For several years, I had been in the process of recording the entire Bible on cassette. It was a monumental project that took me some seven years to complete.

Even though the entire project -- all 66 books of the Old and New Testaments -- are now completed and available ... I could not breathe easy until it was all completed.

The cassettes could never be processed from the master tapes until every word, pronunciation and syllable was checked, rehearsed, and narrated so every "jot and tittle" was perfectly clear and correct. This was both mentally and physically exhausting, but in the end ... fulfilling.

In fact, not too long ago we were given an award to commemorate the distribution of over one million of the NIV Bible cassettes. It's almost hard to envision that many tapes of God's Word being heard by so many people.

Someone told me that packed in cartons of 500 audio cassettes, a million Bible tapes would fill over 100 40-foot semi-trailer trucks!

There were times of difficulty and discouragement during those seven years it took to produce the series, but the genuine satisfaction that came as a result of completing the task was well worth all the effort.

It reminds me of a story I heard about the famous Italian artist and sculptor.

One of Michelangelo's famous statues is only half finished, because the marble was found to be imperfect. He wanted to "liberate the figure imprisoned in the stone". Each time he began to sculpt a figure ... he refused to be satisfied with any piece of marble of inferior quality, or with a lesser work of art.

His disappointment is reflected in that unfinished statue -- and we share his disappointment at not being able to see a completed work of art.

The human race could well be called "God's Great Disappointment." Unlike Michelangelo's imperfect piece of marble, God's original creation was perfect. But that perfect creation -- man -- carried within a flaw and imperfection called sin.

The cross of Christ is designed to bring out our very best! He doesn't wink at sin. Through Jesus' sacrifice, we're made perfect ... despite our defects.

Fortunately, He's still sculpting us. Someday soon, the finishing touch will be made ... and the unveiling will finally take place ... when we're with Him in Eternity.

> "For we are His workmanship, created in Christ Jesus unto good works..." (Ephesians 2:10)

RELEASE

Someone cut me off in my car today. It wasn't that much of a deal -- and was over in just a few seconds. But I steamed about it all day long. And the more I thought about it, the angrier I got.

Then my imagination took over and I thought of what I'd do if I saw that fellow again. I must admit it was not a pretty picture.

So maybe I should not have been too surprised that I was grumpy with co-workers and friends. Or that I didn't feel like eating. Or that I had a headache before I went to bed.

I learned something today: that thoughts are real things. And when I am tied-up emotionally to negative thoughts, I become a prisoner to them. Anger, for example, hardly ever affects the person for whom we harbor these terrible thoughts. They only eat away at our own well being and peace of mind.

We must have control over the things we think and the scenes we picture in our minds. Let's remember to consciously release our thoughts from the negative.

> "Finally, brethren, whatsoever things are true, whatsoever things are honest, whatsoever things are just, whatsoever things are pure,

whatsoever things are lovely,
whatsoever things are of good
report; if there be any virtue, and if
there be any praise, think on these
things."   (Philippians 4:8)

THE GREATEST WONDER

1. The Pyramids of Egypt

2. The Hanging Gardens of Babylon

3. The Statue of Zeus

4. The Temple of Diana at Ephesus

5. The Mausoleum of Halicarnassus

6. The Colossus of Rhodes

7. The Pharos

These constitute what historically have been
classified as the "Seven Great Wonders of the
World." Of these ancient treasures, only one
remains today -- The Pyramids.

However, I believe that there is another
great wonder of the world that far eclipses all
other wonders. This greatest of all wonders is
"The Empty Tomb of Jesus." Of all the world's

great religious leaders, only one has defeated death and brings us promise of eternal life.

Isn't it fascinating how we, as human beings, are able to settle for something far less than what God has given? This has been true ever since the deception of Adam and Eve in Eden.

Paul was right on target when he said, "The god of this world hath blinded the minds of them which believe not, lest the light of the glorious Gospel of Christ, Who is the image of God, should shine unto them" (2 Corinthians 4:4).

Many of us can point to something which could be a great wonder in our little world. NIGHTSOUNDS is one such wonder in my life and ministry ... and even more so, the fact that we are entering our 20th Anniversary year!

And looking beyond our own personal wonders I'm filled with gratitude and praise when I see responses to the broadcast, and especially when I see the many wonders God has worked in so many lives.

So, let's just add to those seven historical wonders of the world our own spiritual wonders, and continue to praise Him "whose mercies are new every morning ..."

"... Great and marvellous are
thy works, Lord God Almighty ..."
(Revelation 15:3)

GOING FOR THE GOLD

If you happened to see one of the women's gymnastic finals in the 1992 Summer Olympic Games at Barcelona recently, perhaps you noticed the young Russian athlete who won the gold medal, but who, moments before her winning effort, had sat alone weeping. Later, a young American man won the gold, and he, too, was so overcome with the intensity of the physical and emotional output that he all but collapsed in tears. They showed their humanity.

Momentarily, the intricacies and sorrow of war, dissent, foreign policy-making and politics were pre-empted by these two athletes.

In their emotional responses, they de-polarized people of all nations by their humanity and, as a result, were the most effective ambassadors that their respective governments could have had at that point.

Many people are trying to win the contest against the stress areas of their lives: depression, loneliness, unemployment, marital problems, the death of a loved one, or even one's own sanity. We need to be reminded of the encouragement of the Paul the Apostle, to stay in the race and stretch for the goal in the name of Christ our Sovereign.

You and I, even through our tears -- whether of victory or defeat -- are ambassadors of Jesus Christ (2 Corinthians 5:20). Yes, even in the restrictive bondage of trauma, we are representatives of the King, just as Paul was "an ambassador in bonds" (Ephesians 6:20).

I don't know what the music of Heaven will be like, but some day the moment of victory will arrive and we will stand in the winner's circle with exultant, tear-filled eyes and sing the anthem of Heaven. I have a feeling that it might even eclipse the magnificent "Hallelujah Chorus." So be it! Let's go "for the gold"!

> "… forgetting those things which are behind, and reaching forth unto those things which are before, I press toward the mark for the prize of the high calling of God in Christ Jesus."
>
> (Philippians 3:13,14)

BELONGING

The little tear-stained face had the look of almost unbelieving panic as her eyes darted from one adult face to another. But none looked familiar to her and you could see the small girl's growing sense of fear as the thousands of holiday travelers were energetically making their ways to or from flights at this, the world's busiest airport, O'Hare International in Chicago.

The child began to cry for her parents. At once the sound of her cries began to rise above the din of the crowd. Then, suddenly, a hand reached down. Strong arms grasped her, and she was swung up into her daddy's arms and drawn back into the circle of love and protection where she belonged.

It seems that each of us has an innate need to belong.

We're "wired" to experience a certain type of intimacy: to know and be known, to love and to be loved, to have friends, to share, to give and receive.

In my high school days I felt uncomfortably disconnected from other students because I was quiet, somewhat invisible and only noticed when I happened to play a trombone solo in assembly or with the band. I needed the band; I had no separate identity.

The Body of Jesus Christ doesn't accept

only certain persons into its ranks, such as apostles, prophets, evangelists, teachers, etc. We all have some gift within us that we can give back to Him with interest. Whatever your gift (public, private, great or small), you belong to the Body. God Himself will take care of your needs for fulfillment and esteem, in His time.

Sometimes we need reassurance, though, don't we? God says that you and I, as His blood-bought children, are heirs of His, but perhaps we need more than a reminder:

> You belong to God if Christ is in your life! (Acts 2:44-47)
> You are a gifted person! (Romans 12:6)
> You are part of the Body of Christ! (1 Cor. 12:13)
> You belong! (1 Cor. 3:23)
> You are accepted! (Romans 15:7)
> When this news actually begins to sink in, it could even make your day! (Philippians 4:4)

DO THE DEAD SPEAK?

Anyone who has lost a loved one -- who has seen a treasured life slip into the shadow of death -- knows both the silence and loneliness and grief. And, it can happen in an instant.

It may be that death has even touched your family, friends, or social circle this past year.

We're not inclined to think of death, so it comes uninvited, and usually without warning. So we try to ignore it.

We look back at yesterday when life seemed complete, if not perfect. Doors were opened, goodbyes were followed by reunions. But now, suddenly life is broken in two -- doors are slammed shut and it all seems so final.

I recall the death of a young man in his thirties who worked with us at NIGHTSOUNDS. He died of cancer several years ago. Yet, it is hard to believe one so young could die. And maybe it's a form of denial, but often I think I see this man driving the car in the next lane, or in a crowd. Can it be that he's alive? But it's only someone who resembles him.

Without a doubt there is a universal finality in death. Yet, some of the lonely hold on ... but they become vulnerable.

Some, in their vulnerability, will do anything to restore that living link. They may even try suicide as a means of joining their loved one. Some actually try to contact the dead -- as if this might somehow increase their own faith.

But instead, it's likely to open up a hornet's nest. To give credence to such scams and other occult expressions is a dead-end experience.

We must face the truth. The dead have met their appointment. It is time for us, the living, to move on.

Our answers are found among the living.

The late Theodore Epp said, "Your concept of death will determine your philosophy of life."

"Love is strong as death..."
(Song of Solomon 8:6)

"Yea, though I walk through the valley of the shadow of death, I will fear no evil; for thou art with me..." (Psalms 23:4)

THE FUTURE IS HERE!

Following a concert appearance in a midwestern city, a young handsome black man approached me and asked, "Some night on NIGHTSOUNDS, would you consider speaking on the subject of 'The Future', because I don't see any future for me?"

The conversation shifted to other matters, and he moved on. But those words lingered and bounced around in my mind and spirit. It occurred to me that we do indeed have a future. Everyone has.

The question is: "What kind of future?"

Also: "Where and how will it be spent?"

Have you ever considered that you are the greatest person that anyone could be? Think about that for a moment. Let it sink into your consciousness: you are the greatest person that anyone can be. Not because you are perfect, but because you are a child of God!

The problem with that is not everyone is a child of God. There is a prerequisite to that position. But the good news is there is no one reading these lines who cannot become a child of God by faith in Jesus Christ at this very moment!

Some years ago, an outcast beggar was sitting in a doorway of a vacant building. Apparently a homeless vagrant, the man had stationed himself across the street from an artist's

51

studio. The artist, seeing the man sit there day after day, took notice of him and began to paint his portrait.

When the picture was finished, he called over to the beggar to come across the street and look at it.

At first the beggar was reluctant, then cautiously made his way to where the artist stood. Amazingly, he didn't recognize himself.

"Who is it?" he asked.

The artist smiled but said nothing. As the beggar kept staring at the painting, recognition slowly began to dawn. Hesitantly he asked, "It is me?"

The artist nodded, as the vagrant shook his head. "Can that really be me?"

The artist replied, "That is the man I see in you."

The beggar looked at the portrait quietly for another moment, then stood up straight, and made a wonderful reply.

"If that's the man you see, "he said to the artist," then that's the man I'll be!"

The future does not always have to be so uncertain. We can take control of our future and make something great of it.

> "O that they were wise, that
> they understood this, that they
> would consider their latter end!
>   (Deuteronomy 32:29)

HAZARDOUS OCCUPATIONS

Demolition Worker ... Policeman ... Fireman ... Fighter Pilot ... Minister.

What do all of these people have in common? They're all engaged in hazardous occupations.

The minister? -- a hazardous occupation? Maybe you've never thought about your pastor as being engaged in a hazardous occupation.

Your minister is actually involved in a vocation filled with stress and spiritual conflict. He's often caught up in counseling where he must allow himself to be vulnerable. Ironically, the Hollywood media often portray the minister either as a stupid and unsophisticated clod or as a wimpy, colorless person of no strength or personality. But neither stereotype fits the reality of the situation.

Stupid? Wimpy? Nothing could be further from the truth! The minister has brains and strength. How else could he open himself to Satan's worst offensive?.

But all those in any hazardous occupations can feel safe if they know Who is at the center of their life.

If God is at the center, the circumference will take care of itself.

> "For in the time of trouble,
> He shall hide me ..."(Psalms 27:5)

RESCUE STATION

Years ago, on a dangerous seacoast, there was a lighthouse that warned of dangerous reefs and treacherous tides. And in the ground level of the lighthouse was a rescue station. Little more than a crude room, it provided relief for the lost and floundering. Many were saved. And the little rescue station became well-known.

In fact, it's successes brought all kinds of local attention and even a great many financial contributions.

Soon there were new rescue boats. Then new beds replaced the old cots, then new furnishings, and a strange opulence. The old rescue station became sort of a popular gathering place.

Before long members grew fuzzy about their purpose and no longer went on rescue missions. They hired crews who specialized in this duty.

If you visit that seacoast today, you'll find an exclusive club located in the base of that lighthouse where once there was a rescue station. But don't visit by way of the sea, because shipwrecks still are frequent -- and boats break up ... people drown. Lives are lost, because those in the rescue station are no longer focused on their mission.

Well, that's a quaint allegory. But the fact

is, churches, support groups, even families can be like this rescue station. Complacent. Jaded. Putting pretense over content. In doing so, we lose our original purpose. We forfeit our mission … and are no longer the light and hope for those who are lost.

> "I urge you therefore, brethren, by the mercies of God, to present your bodies a living and holy sacrifice, acceptable to God, which is your spiritual service of worship. And do not be conformed to this world, but be transformed by the renewing of your mind, that you may prove what the will of God is, that which is good and acceptable and perfect."(Romans 12:1,2, NAS)

DECISIONS, DECISIONS

Today, at a certain time and place, I made an intellectual decision to turn the steering wheel of my car to the left so that I would be heading south on Forest Hills Road, instead of turning to the right and going north.

That simple action made a huge difference in my day. Even though there were other routes I could have used to arrive at the NIGHTSOUNDS studio, I still -- ultimately -- would have had to turn south from my starting location.

A simple action, a simple decision, but it was important.

Most of us live as if the world is predictable in many ways. We walk confidently as if the ground won't crumble under out next step. We make plans as if the sun will rise again tomorrow at about the same time.

We tend to relate to others as if they won't change, become violent, pull out a gun and start shooting.

Our "as if" assumptions do influence our present happiness and our future.

It doesn't follow then, as some people would say, that it doesn't matter what you believe as long as you believe something. But all roads do not lead to be same place! There is no way we can be forever neutral in life. Sooner or later we begin to see the consequences resulting from our decisions. Some of our decisions yield results immediately; others longer, but the law of cause and effect is at work.

The Bible is replete with conditions. The word "if" is often seen. This word hangs over the head of each person; there is ultimate accountability to God.

This is not a threat. Rather, it's an open, loving invitation to make a decision for or against Jesus Christ. We cannot remain neutral toward Him because He did not remain neutral toward us.

> "... choose you this day whom ye will serve; whether the gods which your fathers served that were on the other side ... but as for me and my house, we will serve the Lord." (Joshua 24:15)

OUT OF MY MIND

A nation of fifty million people followed a madman. They listened to Adolph Hitler, not only with their ears but with their emotions, their feelings. What led them to this Nazi ruin? How could sensible human beings permit Hitler's horrible atrocities? Perhaps when they came to hear their leader ... the Germans checked their minds at the door. How else can rational people explain it?

Nearly half a century later, an African admirer of Hitler, Idi Amin, was every bit as murderous, yet a world watched without intervention. What were they thinking?

A few years later, hundreds entered Jonestown, Guyana, and followed a misguided religious leader, Jim Jones, with all of their hearts. They demonstrated their absolute allegiance to him by swallowing poison with him.

What happened -- had they checked their minds at the door?

Christians are often criticized for accepting God's truth by faith. Yet, this is not to say we have set aside our intelligence. The problem is complicated even more as well meaning but spiritually seeking yet uninformed people tell us that intelligence gets in the way of faith -- that somehow, if you process your beliefs intellectually as well as emotionally and spiritually, your mind will somehow short circuit your faith. We are told, in essence, "Check your mind at the door."

Yet God calls on us to renew or minds, (Romans 12:2); to use our intellect wisely. Our destiny depends on it. In the words of Dr. John Stott, "The only alternative to a renewed mind is conformity to the world."

"Set your mind on the things above ..." (Colossians 3:2)

"Let the word of Christ richly dwell within you, with all wisdom teaching and admonishing one another ..." (Colossians 3:16)

BE A GOOD NEIGHBOR

neigh-bor/'na-ber/n   1: one living or
located near another 2: fellowman

It occurred to me the other day that I don't
know the name of the person who has lived next
door to me for the three years I have lived in
Rockford.

It's true that our life-styles, working hours,
and personalities are entirely different, so it's not
always easy to meet people and become more
acquainted with them. Yet, I feel a bit ashamed
that I don't know my neighbor and will try to
remedy the situation as soon as I can.

I read on account an elderly woman who
had lived amid many neighbors in a low-rent
apartment complex. No one paid much attention
to her. No one was even aware that she had died
one day in her small apartment, alone.

Jesus said, "Love your neighbor as
yourself." I'm not sure He meant simply those
who live next door. Yes, these too. But more
likely he meant those who live and work beside us.
I believe He wanted us to consider these resolves:

-- I will use the language of gentleness
and not words that bite or tones that
crush;
-- I will practice patience;

-- I will remember that my neighbors have burdens enough to carry without loading them with mine;

-- I will excuse others' faults and failures as often and as fully as I expect them to be lenient with mine;

-- I will trade criticism for commendation;

-- I will gladden my nature by smiling out loud and freely using the "magic" words of "Please", "Thank you", and "You're terrific!" if they fit.

The practice of these suggestions creates "soil" for further seed-sowing of our faith in Christ. If we can be good neighbors, just maybe someone will listen to what we have to say!

> "You have heard that it was said, 'You shall love your neighbor and hate your enemy.' But I say to you, love your enemies, and pray for those who persecute you."
> (Matthew 5:43, 44 NAS)

REACHING FOR LOVE

A grieving father couldn't bear the tragic loss of his only daughter, so he took his own life. He couldn't cope with the thought of living in an impersonal world without the one he loved so much.

This father's suicide only compounded the tragedy. It's really too bad that another family member or friend did not sense his grief and come to his rescue.

Most of us would have helped that father if we had only known. The problem is, most people like this father, don't wear obvious signs on them making them identifiable. They're disguised behind ordinary or even expressionless faces, masks that are deceptive, as fake as a circus clown.

These people are locked into loneliness because they don't know how to break out of that prison. To them, the only way out, seems to be the bottom of a bottle, the end of a needle, or -- in the case of this grief stricken dad, the muzzle of a gun.

We pass by them every day, but we don't really see them.

Still, how many of us can love the masses? But, it should be a lofty goal -- to reach out to hurting individuals -- souls with deep and tragic pain -- with the love of the God-Man Who walked the earth two thousand years ago. It was He who looked out at the multitude ... and was moved with compassion.

> "The Lord is compassionate
> and gracious, slow to anger and
> abounding in loving kindness. He
> has not dealt with us according to
> our sins ... Just as a father has com-
> passion on his children, so the Lord
> has compassion on those who fear
> Him." (Psalms 103:8,10,13 NAS)

ARE YOU FOR REAL?

Sometime back, one of our forthright and refreshingly candid teenage listeners began her letter to me with the question, "Are you for real?

Her comments continued, "So many religious speakers on radio and TV sound slightly unreal to me. I was wondering if you were a little 'phoney' too."

My initial reaction was, "Well, if I am, I sure don't want anyone to find out!"

Actually she was referring to a few media preachers who had fallen, but still tried to sound pious to their audiences. Yet, I was thinking of less carnal flaws. So I began a genuine inventory of soul and motive.

It really did help me to "clean house" in my spirit. I began to spot-check certain broadcast tapes, to see if I could detect any hint of insincerity or doubt in the body of the program that might produce suspicion of its credibility -- in either content or delivery.

To my surprise, I did encounter an occasional statement or song lyric that could be construed as somewhat unrealistic -- maybe a little too flippant, naive or sentimental.

There are times when even the Word of God sounds a bit incredible, because we have not come into contact with its reality. Maybe it seems almost too far from our grasp. Yet, when we "connect" with the Bible by faith, and ask the Spirit of God to make us real, we begin to develop a credible philosophy of life.

Then, strangely enough, we are motivated by God's Grace; we are taught by the Holy Spirit, doing everything within His power to conform our lives to God's plan.

Remember, the only liberty we really have is our liberty to choose a master.

So, the immediate answer to the question, "Are you a 'phoney'?" is, basically, "Yes, a little, sometimes."

However, I'm enrolled in a tough, but effective course in God's classroom called "Discipling" and I'm actually learning to be FOR REAL!

> "... He who began a good work in you will carry it on to completion until the day of Christ Jesus"   (Philippians 1:6 NIV).

FIRE AND WATER

The vast majority of my mail deals with letters of deep stress and pain. The compounded hurt is sometimes too intense and I must put the letters aside until the Lord gives me the ability to read and prayerfully enter into the agony of which they write.

Do you ever feel as though you're being "tried by fire" or buffeted by the great emotional storm? And when the pain strikes, do you ever wonder, "Why me?"

The French painter Andre Matisse once watched the master Pierre Auguste Renoir, paint in his old age. It was almost too hard for Matisse to bear as he watched Renoir, his fingers pained and crippled by arthritis, work so meticulously at the canvas.

"Why do you continue?" Matisse asked.

Renoir thoughtfully replied, "Because the pain passes. The beauty remains." The master artist had learned that there are qualities that transcend even pain.

You see, any time you go through the fire and water of adversity, God has a reason for it. Or, as the author of old couplet has written:

Every falsehood that is said,
Every teardrop that is shed,
There is a reason.

But, if we trust Him
As we should ...
All will work out for our good.

> "And we know that all things
> work together for good to them that
> love God, to them who are called
> according to His purpose."
> (Romans 8:28)

THERE'S GOOD NEWS TONIGHT

Are you old enough to remember the voice of commentator Gabriel Heater on the radio during the 1940's? His trademark introduction was the phrase, "Ah, there's good news tonight!"

There are many who long for that kind of news. I'd be happy if I only had ..."

Fill in the blank. What would make you happy? A better job? More money? A spouse?

Maybe some people might actually be happier if they had those things ... but, for how long? I've heard a lot of people complain: "Oh, if only I had done that job better, studied better, or taken this or that action, I'd be happier."

But look at Jesus' words in the Beatitudes: "Happy are those that ..." well, you ought to be

able to fill in the blanks.   Remember, Jesus'
emphasis in on believing, receiving, obeying.

Ironically, happiness is not based on things.

Personal happiness is a state of being --- a
choice. Choosing happiness, even in tough times,
fills the heart.

Now that you know where to find
happiness, why not choose it for yourself?

"But seek ye first the kingdom
of God, and His righteousness, and
all these things shall be added unto
you."   (Matthew 6:33)

DO YOU MATTER?

I saw the construction of a building going up near the Cherry Vale shopping mall in the city where I live. On closer inspection, the sign out front informs passersby that a new restaurant is being built called T.G.I.F.

I was told that it was a franchise restaurant and that the initials stood for "Thank God It's Friday". Can you imagine, living six days a week looking forward to only one?

It's not unusual. Many people live for the weekend. They dread Mondays. They're bored.

What about you? Would you work at your occupation even if you weren't getting paid for it? That is, is there any meaning beyond the paycheck? Boredom is a danger signal that your life may need refocusing. Perhaps you need to reset your goals ... assuming, of course, that you even have them.

You see, what you do matters because <u>you matter.</u> We all need to matter ... to mean something to someone, to relate meaningfully to some project, to some ideal.

Dedication to a vision, a higher goal, gives significance to our lives ... and it chases boredom.

Our needs as human beings transcend the physical. Jesus reminded us of that fact most clearly when He said, "Man does not live by bread alone."

> "For God so loved the world,
> that He gave His only begotten Son,
> that whosoever believeth in Him
> should not perish, but have
> everlasting life." (John 3:16)

CHRISTIAN YELLOW PAGES

I ran into a curious thing the other day. It was a directory listing the names, addresses and phone numbers of Christian businesses in the area. The display ads had little "fish" emblems, doves, crosses and other symbols of faith.

There are a lot of businesses these days linking themselves with their owners' religious roots. You've seen them, as they're identified right in the name: Christian Bookstores, Christian Auto Dealerships, various Christian services -- even Christian Hair Designers.

Anything wrong with that? No, not necessarily -- but I got to thinking how it takes more than a religious symbol or logo to make a business Christian.

For example, can the public expect better service from a Christian Dry Cleaner?.

Can shoppers expect a better environment in which to shop? What about integrity? Do

Christian businessmen pay their bills on time? How truthful is their advertising? Can they be trusted?

We must be careful. Our caution is not just how we work with or treat other Christians who might trade with the Christian business. But there's a more important clientel watching with interest, and because so many cynics are watching, this is why we must be so careful. The skeptics who work with a Christian business want to "see" a sermon not hear one.

It may seem like a harsh standard, but, after all, the name implication -- to call yourself a Christian in any context -- demands honesty and commitment.

> "And whatsoever ye do in word or deed, do all in the name of the Lord Jesus ...
>
> And whatsoever ye do, to it heartily, as unto the Lord ..."
> (Colossians 3:17,23)

WHAT NEXT?

Mid-life crises ... job lay-off ... sudden tragedy ... career change ... forced retirement. Any one of these factors could send a person into an emotional tailspin. Life's changes are often difficult to handle. And even if we don't face any of the drastic conditions listed above, to one degree or another, the question, "What next?" still hovers over each of us.

I can imagine the disciples of Jesus, after responding to His call to "Follow," began each day with the thought, "What next?" or "Where do we go from here?" They had the choice of facing the next day with either dread or trust. And so do we who follow Him.

Often we are compelled to "road test" the Scriptural instruction to "walk by faith, not by sight." I'm sure that Joni Eareckson Tada never dreamed, as she lay on that hospital bed totally paralyzed, what was "next" for her as an invalid. Yet, she was raised up through her difficulty to have an international ministry to millions.

I'm also reminded of Jim Elliot and four of his college buddies who went as missionaries to the Auca Indians in Ecuador some 30 years back, inspired by Amy Carmichael's prayer, "Make me Thy fuel, flame of God." They all gave their lives the afternoon they arrived at the Auca Village -- before they had even invested very much of their

time and talents for God.   Yet, through their
deaths, many Indians were converted while countless others worldwide gave their lives to
missionary service. How shall we respond?

There is the apocryphal epitaph found on a
country gravestone:

> "Died at fifty,
> Buried at seventy,
> Died of hardening of
> the viewpoints."

So, if "attitude determines destiny," the
"what's nexts" of our lives are best handled
through the good word of counsel from God's en-
ergetic apostle named Paul, and another apostle,
John, who wrote to all of us:

> "Don't worry about anything;
> instead, pray about everything; tell
> God your needs and don't forget to
> thank Him for His answers. If you
> do this, you will experience God's
> peace, which is far more wonderful
> than the human mind can under-
> stand.   His peace will keep your
> thoughts and your hearts quiet and
> at rest as you trust in Christ Jesus"
> (Philippians 4:6-7, LB).

> "In this act we see what real
> love is: It is not our love for God,

73

but His love for us when He sent His son to satisfy God's anger against our sins." (1 John 4:10)

STORM WARNING!

As this is being written, the TV newscasts are filled with the dramatic and tragic aftermath of hurricane Andrew following its devastating path across Southern Florida, and another terrible hurricane hitting one of the Hawaiian islands.

This seems to be quite a season for storms. Do storms frighten you? Or, except for those of disastrous proportions such as hurricanes or tornados, do they exhilarate you? It's funny how the same event can be interpreted so differently by so many people.

A storm is a good metaphor for the human race. It usually means going through a tough time, being tossed about by events, wondering if we'll make it home okay.

But storms also water the ground ... clear the air ... and even fertilize the soil through the discharge of nitrogen in lightening. But the most important thing about storms is -- they pass!

Isn't it interesting how we often get the greatest satisfaction from "riding out" these storms of life and the subsequent trying times?

You see, God has never promised to eliminate storms from our lives, What He does offer is His protection and His strength to help us endure them.

> "... Oh that I had wings like a dove! I would fly away and be at rest ... I would hasten to my place of refuge from the stormy wind and tempest ... Cast your burden upon the Lord and He will sustain you..."
> (Psalms 55:6,8,22 NAS)

OVERNIGHT SUCCESS

A recent winner of an Oscar award, who was not particularly well-known to the public, was interviewed after the ceremony. "How does it feel to be an overnight success?" the actor asked.

"Overnight? Yeah, right! My overnight success has taken twenty-five years!"

You see, we saw only his recent movie ... and the acceptance of the award prompted by that motion picture. What we <u>didn't</u> see were the years of school plays, acting school, summer stock theatre and a string of bit parts and commercials. We didn't even know of his experience, his endurance, through the 25 years' "waiting zone."

Yet, this actor had faith in himself. All the rest was part of the "wait" until success found him. And he had learned to make the most of these opportunities along the way.

Let's take advantage of <u>our</u> time in the waiting zone. We can cultivate our prayer life, our expectations, dreams ... and patience. Although our ordinary activities may never be seen by the multitude, there is much we can learn as we move toward the goals we make for our own successes.

And we may surprise a great many people when we get there ... people who will be amazed at our own "overnight" success.

> "If then you have been raised up with Christ, keep seeking the things above ... And whatever you do in word or deed, do all in the name of the Lord Jesus ... do your work heartily, as for the Lord rather than for men; knowing that from the Lord you will receive the reward..."
> (Colossians 3:1,17,23-24 NAS)

BUT, IT HURTS

Remember mercurochrome? Before the era of spray-on disinfectants there was a little bottle of a red liquid that Mom used to patch up the cuts and scratches of little boys ... and tomboys!

She'd wash off the scrape and try to apply the mercurochrome and you'd protest, "But it hurts!"

You'd wince, grit your teeth and wait for the sting to envelop the cut. But you also knew Mom wasn't actually trying to harm you.

In fact, that sting eventually made you better.

We're grown up now. And our scrapes are more emotional than physical. Challenges ... rejections ... heartbreaks ... disappointments.

Why does life hold such hurt? Perhaps if we knew ahead of time that our experiences would make us vulnerable to these scrapes and bruises we'd say, "No, thanks. It's gonna hurt!"

We don't always understand it ... but we trust that even a trial, heartbreak or emotional wound can benefit us. That somehow without it, we would be less complete.

Everything that comes to us in life ... including the hurts ... has purpose and reason, and serves us for our Higher Good.

> "They that sow in tears shall reap in joy. He that goeth forth and weepeth, bearing precious seed, shall doubtless come again with rejoicing..." (Psalms 126:5,6)

WHO'S IN CONTROL?

The mail response to NIGHTSOUNDS brings a variety of questions, needs, and requests. Yet, there are several themes than seem to appear again and again. People write to me of loneliness, fear, worry, or anxiety. So I know that their needs in these areas of human experience are very real.

I believe one of Satan's most successful tools is worry. He often succeeds in getting Christians to fret over even the smallest of circumstances in their lives. Sometimes even the insignificant things seem to pile up and weigh a person down. Satan has become very accomplished at agitating and irritating us ... in the hope that our attention will be diverted from God. Thus diverted, our minds dwell on our troubles and focus only on our problems.

The Psalmist said that we should not fret -- or worry -- that God has control of the circumstances.

The late Robert J. Little, my friend and radio associate, used to say, "Do you think Jesus took the disciples out on the stormy sea to let them drown? Of course not. Neither will the Lord allow you to be overcome."

God told the Apostle Paul that His strength was made perfect in weakness. That is still true today. Worry does not change circumstances. But

God does.

When we face some tense situation, trial, or difficult problem in life we are reminded, "Cast your care upon Him for He careth for you."

In the midst of trouble, do not give in to worry. Rather, hold on to God and His promises, through prayer. Concentrate on the solution rather than the problem.

Let us pray for one another. Prayer is the <u>least</u> <u>used</u> and most important source of power in the world.

> "For the Lord God, the Holy One of Israel, says: Only in returning to Me and waiting for Me will you be saved; in quietness and confidence is your strength ..."
> (Isaiah 30:15 LB)

ARE YOU GETTING OLDER?

I saw a recent birthday card with this humorous advice: "Pushing 50 is all the exercise you need."

The Hallmark stores have all kinds of cards for those who add another year to their life-span. And that includes us all! Aging is a universal experience, yet it's interesting to watch how different people deal with that experience.

Are you alive? Or just living? If you're "just living" you're merely counting the days. But a life that is actively "alive" -- with zip, with zest -- keeps us young.

Well, of course, physically, we are all aging. Still, it's no secret, some of us age better than others ... some of us stay younger longer. Eating well, exercise and other good habits help, too. However, the physical aspect is only one side of the coin. There's a mental side, too.

Many studies indicate that aging is almost like a self-fulfilling prophecy -- a person becomes what he or she expects to become.

So, keep the wide-eyed, wonder-filled child very much alive within you even into your later years!

The real Fountain of Youth is a strong mind ... determined not to grow old in heart, mind, or spirit.

81

> "For me to live is Christ ...
> Let this mind be in you, which was
> also in Christ Jesus... for it is God
> which worketh in you both to will
> and to work for His good pleasure."
> (Philippians 1:21, 2:5,13)

WHAT ARE YOU READING?

I have something before me that I cannot live without. It's a book. Not just any book. It's the one that shows up on the best-seller list every year. It's the book most people say they'd want if they were stranded on a desert island.

It instructs. It corrects. It trains. And it's a privilege to live by its teachings. Of course you've already guessed to which book I refer: the Bible.

Even when viewed simply as literature, this Book is remarkable. It's life-giving and life-sustaining.

So, why is it that so few people read the Bible?

Could it be that it's not easy reading? -- that we have to concentrate? Yes, I'll admit -- reading the Bible can require discipline and demands.

Or, maybe, it's because concentration sounds like work, that we have to dig for meaning and ultimate understanding. But not every prize is easily won. Often the one most difficult goal to attain is the one that we cherish the most.

Don't be discouraged in your daily Bible reading. We need God's Word. As individuals -- and perhaps even more as a society -- we need its light, its discipline, guidance, strength, and encouragement.

> "The entrance of thy words giveth light; it giveth understanding to the simple." (Psalms 119:130)

> "So then faith cometh by hearing, and hearing by the Word of God." (Romans 10:17)

INADEQUATE FOR THE TASK

Have you ever agreed to do something, yet inside felt inadequate for the task? Such was my experience when I was asked to take part in the International Trombone Workshop held yearly at Peabody Teachers College in Nashville.

I knew that many of the people who would be on the program with me were considered real artists of the secular music community. I quietly wondered what I had to offer, since my music had been played only for the glory of God and not performed to impress secular critics.

You may have had experiences like that. A little afraid to relate to non-Christians, yet knowing that if you hid your talent and love for God from them, you'd be falling short of the witness that God wanted you to share.

So, I agreed to do the workshop, but explained that I would confine my verbal and instrument communication to sacred or religious music since this is what I know best. I wondered if they would accept such stipulations, but they agreed.

As the time to go drew near, I found my attitude beginning to change. Instead of fearing this event and feeling inadequate for the task, I developed a desire to play as well as possible and pass along anything I could to the many students I knew would be there. But more than that, I saw an opportunity -- although simple at best -- to communicate the joy I knew in performing music which glorifies Jesus Christ.

Should you be in a similar situation, I urge you to take advantage of any unusual yet simple opportunities to represent the Lord. It may be through showing His spirit of love and kindness at an unkind civic meeting, or your friendly presence at the bedside of a person you hardly know, but have been asked to visit.

There are many ways we can encourage those who don't understand the peace Jesus brings, and we must be willing to do what we can.

In my case, a small nucleus of Christian students on the Peabody campus were praying that Christ would be honored and that the music I came to play would cause those gathered to give earnest heed to the message of Christ. I must admit, I was nervous. I wondered how this ministry would be accepted. To my joy, many of these fine musicians opened up in extensive dialogue. They seemed to be reached in a real way with the lyrics of the hymns and gospel songs.

It is not always in the cloud-splitting or spectacular opportunities, but in the little events that God is blessed and glorified. Your simple opportunity may even go mostly unnoticed, but someone will realize that God is alive if you are faithful.

"Work hard and cheerfully at
all you do, just as though you were
working for the Lord and not

merely for your masters, remembering that it is the Lord Christ who is
going to pay you, giving you your
full portion of all He owns. He is
the one you are really working for."
(Colossians 3:23-24 LB).

WHAT'S IN A NAME?

How did you get your name? Did your
parents pore through a baby-name book before you
were born? Are you named after Grandma? A lot
of youngsters have been given the names of movie
stars, rock performers, popular athletes -- maybe
in the hope that some of the fame and glory
attached to the name might rub off. Perhaps
you're a child with the word "junior" after his
name. That can pose problems -- of living up to
another person's expectations ... or living down
their reputation.

Whatever the situation, your name is a
significant part of your personality. Did you ever
stop to think about that? Whether the origin of
your name is Greek, Roman, or some ancient
dialect, your name has meaning. It's customized
for the challenges, lessons, and joys of your
lifetime. It kind of makes you think that the

angels might have whispered in your parents' ears before you came into this world, because the truth of the matter is -- most people like their name. They are comfortable in hearing it spoken.

But it's something to keep in mind if you're choosing the name of your son or daughter-to-be. Listen to those angelic whispers. It's going to be important to that new soul.

It may seem unimportant on the surface, but I wonder if a child named Elvis, Ringo or Madonna will aspire to the same kind of greatness as a Paul, David or Ruth.

"A good name is rather to be
had than great riches..."
(Proverbs 22:1)

WHO LISTENS?

Who listens to NIGHTSOUNDS?

Perhaps the same lonely, somewhat disoriented, searcher that I was many years ago when I used to tune in a large commercial radio station in Chicago to hear a late night program. I felt I needed that friendly voice and soothing music. The person to whom that voice belonged soon became my friend, although I still had never met him. He made no pretense of being a Christian. His music was secular. He was sponsored by an airline company; but to me even his sales pitch was comforting.

No doubt it was during those lonely nights, that I began to experience the first stirrings in my soul that someday I might be able to talk to people late at night and play beautiful music for them.

(Ironically, some time back, I had an opportunity to sit with this very guy, a great radio talent, in his beautiful studio in Chicago, while he conducted his show. How thrilling it was to hear him tell his listeners about and play our newest recording on his all-night program.)

Because I listened to and was influenced by this top professional announcer, I came away, fired up at least to try -- under God -- to bring, the same high quality performance to the listener, whoever and wherever he or she might be.

And I had an added dimension built on a

discipline of Bible memorization and love of Christian books. This blend struck a chord in the lives of other lonely, seeking persons.

What a challenge it is now to receive mail from busy executives, housewives, college students, the bereaved, the suicidal, the hopeless, those who don't know what to say except "Help!"

This is why -- under God -- we have always wanted to do the best job possible for Him and for all those in need.

So if, in God's divine providence, we should be placed in an area of service or influence, no matter how large or small, let's give it all we have.

> "So, my dear brothers, since future victory is sure, be strong and steady, always abounding in the Lord's work, for you know that nothing you do for the Lord is ever wasted ..."(1 Corinthians 15:58 LB)

WORKAHOLICS

Okay … here's a pop-quiz. You don't need paper or pencil to answer. Just be truthful. Ready? Here it is. Question: How many of your waking hours do you spend with your spouse and family? Figured that out? All right, now.

Next question. What percentage of your time is spent on your work?

It's been shown by studies of typical American families that the average husband, wife and children come together for meaningful conversation and personal interaction less than thirty minutes a day.

No wonder many wives are depressed. Small wonder kids rebel. Their parents' priorities are reversed.

It's so easy to excuse our workaholic behavior -- we are, after all, doing what is "expected" of us. And if we neglect our spouse or children, we explain that it's for them that we work so hard. Yet, if we asked them, we might get an altogether different response.

We think that our work is a means by which we earn the money to feed our families … and certainly that's true as far as "real food" goes.

But emotionally, if you're not feeding your family first, they'll starve .. and so will you!

Only a satisfying and on-going positive emotional relationship at home provides the foundation and fuel for you to serve not just the needs of your family. No, curiously it also gives you the sustenance to deal with the world of your work.

Put God first, feed your family relationships next. And then, after you've given the time to nourish these relationships, you'll find time for work -- and find a new balance for godly living.

"If we confess our sins, he is
faithful and just to forgive us our
sins ...   (1 John 1:9)

THE HAVES AND HAVE-NOTS

Ever thought of being a millionaire? Or in these days of inflation maybe we should dream of being a billionaire. I must confess to brief flights of fantasy when I see the TV commercials for the state lottery. And of course, that's what the lottery officials <u>want</u> you to do -- dream about becoming rich, then going out and buying some lottery tickets to accomplish it.

But such dreams are futile. Gambling your money away on lottery tickets only pushes prudent saving further away.

So, what about it? It is wrong to dream about being rich?

Some people espouse "Prosperity Theology" which says that getting wealth truly demonstrates God's providence and grace.

Others, stressing a Theology of Simplicity, say that the surest way to hell is by accumulating riches; that money corrupts and supplants faith -- that we'd be better to live life simple, without wealth.

Which viewpoint is right?

Well, probably neither. One's happiness doesn't depend on material possessions. And yet there's nothing contradictory about being both spiritual and rich.

But I think that if you have health, employment, loving family and friends, you are already a millionaire, or a billionaire! What do you think?

Actually, your worth depends on what you hold in your heart.

"For where your treasure is,
there will your heart be also."
(Matthew 6:21)

POETRY SAYS IT BEST

From the pen of John Moore:

Create a tender soul in me, oh Lord.
Pierce my heart.
When my vision is distracted,
And my focus seems to blur,
When my will begins to filter out your voice;
When the wounded in the street I hear as
     Just a noisy sound;
When I hesitate to help,
     As if I had a choice ...
From the quiver of your Love
     Let compassion's arrow fly
Speedily toward its target.
Let no obstacles deny
     Its penetrating purpose.
For this life-infusing dart
     Has power to pierce The armor
'Round a cold, indifferent heart.

There are a lot of ways to say, "I love you", though poetry says it best.

"How beautiful upon the mountains are the feet of him that bringeth good tidings, that publisheth peace." (Isaiah 52:7)

93

HOW MUCH IS YOUR
BODY WORTH?

I can remember about 30 years ago a professor from Yale University did a chemical analysis of the human body and said that all its parts were only worth ninety-eight cents!

But times have changed. Now scientists have placed a value on certain human enzymes and hormones that are unique and which cannot be reproduced in the laboratory. These scientists say that even small amounts of these enzymes, hormones and cell components are valued at millions of dollars per gram!

And our complicated network of brain cells, if valued at only five cents a cell, would total one quintillion dollars -- that's one billion billion! That's more money than all the treasuries of all the governments on earth put together. For just the value of one human being!

As the psalmist said, "We are fearfully and wonderfully made." Our Creator gave us a brain that no machine can match. Even in a day and age of superlatives, our bodies are truly a miracle. And we haven't even begun to discuss the value of your <u>soul</u>!

"When I consider thy heavens,
the work of thy fingers, the moon
and the stars, which thou hast

ordained; what is man that thou art mindful of him? ... For thou hast made him a little lower than the angels, and hast crowned him with glory and honor." (Psalms 8:3-5)

SUICIDE

A few weeks ago, our office received a very troubled and troubling letter. It began, "By the time you read this I will be dead." The words were written as a suicide letter by a young man who expressed his despair and deep emotional wounds.

Out entire office personnel were shaken by this act, and we all felt, "What a waste!"

It doesn't sound right ... but the facts are accurate: next to accidents, suicide is the leading cause of death among young adults ages fifteen to twenty-five.

Why? The question seems rhetorical -- no one answers. Still we ask Why? And we grieve. Often we're angry, too. Sometimes, because we weren't sure of the person's spiritual condition we might even hope for the person's soul.

But we shouldn't pass judgment ... yet shouldn't lose hope either.

Many take their lives because they believe them to be worthless, or because they had no one to whom they could turn.

Others are caught up in a despondent moment of hysteria, passion, or even insanity.

How should someone evaluate or judge such an irrational act?

The Scripture reminds us: "Where sin abounds ... grace abounds that much more."

> "Weeping may endure for a night, but joy cometh in the morning." (Psalms 30:5)

> "To all who mourn in Israel He will give:
> Beauty for ashes;
> Joy instead of mourning;
> Praise instead of heaviness."
> (Isaiah 61:3 LB)

LISTEN

Listening is an art form. Of course, it helps if our ears are good, in order that we might hear the sounds. Sound waves moving air molecules across our ear drums. That's <u>hearing</u> -- and hearing is not necessarily the same as listening.

But listening is more than that. Listening means we <u>understand</u> what someone is <u>really</u> communicating to us.

And actually, listening has as much to do with eyes as it does with ears. Think about it. People "speak" in visual cues and other signals all the time: body language, eye movement, tone of voice -- all have a story all their own to "tell." And, that story may not match the words coming out of the mouth!.

You can learn to become a good listener, through practice. Simply go into the silence … and pray. But this time, don't do any of the talking. Just listen. You may find this art of communication with God to be the most rewarding of all.

> "So then faith cometh by hearing, and hearing by the Word of God."   (Romans 10:17)
> "I have heard from the Lord God of hosts … Give ye ear, and

hear My voice; hearken, and hear
My speech.   (Isaiah 28:22,23)

WHAT DO YOU SAY?

Sometimes when I'm in a crowded area, such as O'Hare's busy airport, I often overhear little pieces of conversation. Sometimes I'm offended or embarrassed by what I hear. As a former Marine, I've heard these words before in the barracks, but I'm still uncomfortable to hear them. It's even more distressing somehow to hear them come from the mouths of young women or children.

When we watch movies these days, we're not surprised to hear some off-color words. Even the TV networks are pushing at the barriers and each new TV season introduces a few more obscenities.

But does it have to be so pervasive? And so often?

It reminds me of a recent Time magazine article referring to "America's Foul-Mouthed Pop-Culture." It must be worth reviewing when even the liberal press stops to consider such swearing.

You know, words are like sculpting tools.

They shape our communication. They have a certain resonance, evoke a certain feel. And when they're misused, they lose their value. They compromise our message.

I wonder what some people say these days when they strike their thumb with a hammer? They probably don't know a good common inoffensive word to let out the steam!

Choose your words carefully. They have a shame or dignity all their own. Respect them and they will lend you their power to communicate.

> "A good man thinks before he speaks; the evil man pours out his evil words without a thought."
> (Proverbs 15:28 LB)

THE GUILTY CAN'T SLEEP

Some time ago we received an anonymous letter with a small money order inside. The writer said, in essence, that the money order was a contribution to God's work and was being sent because the writer was unable to sleep at night due to some sin in his or her past. The writer concluded the letter with, "If I am still not able to sleep, I'll send another money order."

Well, we chuckle at that. But some people really want to ease their consciences. In fact, the U.S. government has gotten into the matter.

In case you didn't read about it, Uncle Sam provides a "Conscience Fund" so you can make up any taxes you might not have sent, either because you lied or cheated on your taxes. No questions are asked. Just send your money to the IRS Conscience Fund. Last year, payments ranged from forty-four cents to fifty thousand dollars.

It no doubt lightened the burden. Oh, not just the government's. The taxpayer's too! All those guilty minds are now clear. They'll find it much easier to sleep at night.

And for at least one person, paying fifty thousand dollars was apparently easier than being constantly tormented by guilt. Guilt frustrates our desire to be at peace. It also destroys self--

confidence, self-esteem and relationships.

And worst of all, guilt drives us away from the source who can deliver us ... a loving God who says, "You are forgiven."

> "If we confess our sins, He is faithful and just to forgive us our sins, and to cleanse us from all unrighteousness." (1 John 1:9)

DO MEN NEED FRIENDS?

Are you an adult American male?

Well, something's missing in your life.

You see, studies and surveys show that the typical American male relies too much on the stereotype: macho, independent, tough, and distant. These studies show that the typical adult American male is generally uncommunicative ... and friendless. Oh, he has a number of acquaintances. But for the most part, men lack close, satisfying male relationships in their lives.

It seems that women have close, deep friendships and are able to share their most intimate thoughts and problems with another woman.

But men, somewhat protective and afraid

to demonstrate their feelings, hesitate to reach out for male friendship and sharing.

Yet, the experts remind us that it is important for men to have close personal friendships. They tell us that "male bonding" is also important ... and not just on the golf course or at business lunches.

When men share deeply held, basic beliefs, an intimate, long-term relationship can emerge. And men who need other men, grow more emotionally complete.

> "I will try to walk a blameless path, but how I need your help, especially in my own home, where I long to act as I should."
> (Psalms 101:2 LB)

THE TYRANNY OF
THE URGENT

The direction and dimensions of this chapter took on some fascinating proportions and actually began a number of years ago as I began to write these thoughts originally as the lead article for a NIGHTSOUNDS newsletter.

I began and concluded three different ways in as many minutes. I'd started with two potential topics yet both of them dissipated, because I decided to write while sitting beside my seven-year-old son. Randy said he was scared and couldn't sleep, so I sat in his bedroom to reassure him while trying to write.

As my thoughts were taking form, Randy began to ask questions:

"Dad, when I think about God sometimes I start thinking about Satan, too. That bothers me. Does that ever happen to you?" Then, before I could reply, another question.

"Why did God let Satan hate Him and fight against Him?" And then, "How many angels does Satan have?" By now Randy wasn't even waiting for an answer. His questions just tumbled out. "How were we born? Why does Jesus love little children?"

After pausing to catch his breath, he said, "I thought you said you were going to write something. Why aren't you writing?"

I smiled and answered, "Because I'm thinking it's more important to answer your good questions than for me to write just now!"

"The Tyranny of the Urgent" was a title I noticed on a booklet one time. As Randy had fired off his questions, my mind flashed back to that phrase. As the deadline for my newsletter column was crowding me with its urgency, I had hoped to write something impressive about spiritual discipline, music forms, or some other topic.

Yet, for some strange, but familiar reason certain priorities began to assume a proper sequence in my mind. It would have been much more convenient and efficient to say nicely, but firmly to Randy, "I can't talk to you now; I'm busy writing. Now go to sleep!"

I'm glad I did not allow the urgent to crowd out the important.

Isn't it good that God doesn't give us a terse answer like that when we need His fellowship or are afraid?

Instead, His responses are:

"Come to me ... I will give you rest."
"Let not your heart be troubled."
"My grace is sufficient for you ... my strength is made perfect in weakness."
"Neither do I condemn you."
"I have loved you with an everlasting love."
"I will never leave you nor forsake you."

CONTRADICTIONS

Lots of things seem on the surface to make sense ... but they're incorrect. Like:

Meekness is weakness.
Money buys anything.
The loudest talker is the most persuasive.
Men are impressed only with a pretty face.
You have to be aggressive to get ahead.
Brute force always wins.
Etc.

The ultimate model of wonderful contradictions is the powerful kindness is God. He does not have to be stimulated to greater power by competition with His friends or His enemies.

Actually, the Bible is a book of such reversals of apparent logic. Who would have predicted that the long-awaited Messiah would appear in a stable behind our backs? We would have looked for Him by gazing into the sky, awaiting a gold chariot heralded by a celestial trumpets.

We would never guess that this One would have "nowhere to lay His head" while His representatives flashily live in the finest homes and condos?

Who of us would have ever imagined that

He would leave with anything less than the most elaborate funeral preparations, attended by royalty from all lands?

It's just not logical.

Like electricity, God's divine grace, like His love, is accepted by faith. We'll never understand it, but we can still experience it. It just doesn't make sense. But it works!

> "For the wisdom of this world is foolishness before God."
> (1 Corinthians 3:18)

JESUS IN THE LOCKER ROOM

As I walked through the cavernous tunnel that was part of the underside of Wrigley Field, home of the Chicago Cubs, I again began to feel a vague sense of uneasiness. It happens almost every time I am called upon to appear as a chapel speaker for a major league baseball team or one of our nation's great professional football clubs.

Sam Bender, Midwest coordinator of the National Baseball Chapel Ministries, met me just before the Cubs game with a big smile, firm handshake and these words: "I'm sure glad it's you, not me, who is speaking to the Dodgers this morning. That Los Angeles club is a tough one!"

My heart sank a little and I slowed my pace. "Why is that?"

"Oh, probably pride," he responded. "They're a good team. Maybe it's just a 'Hollywood' cockiness."

As Sam continued, I listened, but inwardly prayed at the same time: "Lord, who am I? I've got nothing to say to people like those baseball 'superstars'. Please help me, as you gave the right words to David, Daniel, and Paul."

My confidence began to come back as I remembered -- the bottom line is that God honors His Word. He was there with me, as He always is at our point of need ... making His strength perfect in our weakness.

It can be very intimidating to talk to baseball teams like the Cubs, Dodgers, Yankees and Reds ... or the football clubs like the Bears, Packers, Steelers, and Oilers. Yet one message always reaches me at those moments: "There are no superstars at the foot of the cross of Jesus Christ." At each man's moment of death, our only "claim to fame" is the sacrifice of Jesus Christ.

The World Series, or the Super Bowl, great as they are, are inconsequential events compared to the act of accepting Jesus as Lord and Savior.

Who is the Superstar? It is the One who has overcome the world.

And the wonderful follow-up to that great idea is the fact that Jesus has given this unique Power to His followers:

> "Truly, truly, I say to
> you, he who believes in Me, the
> works that I do shall he do also; and
> greater works than these shall he do
> ... If you ask Me anything in my
> name, I will do it."
> (John 14:12,14 NAS)

FREE AT LAST!

Most of us are in bondage to one degree or another to something or someone. Maybe this is because we don't realize how free we can be. Paul the Apostle reminded believers that since Christ set us free, to be free men, we must stand firm, then, and refuse to be tied to the yoke of slavery. (Galatians 5:1).

Paul wrote this to the Galatians who were slaves to fears, superstitions, passions, and baser human instincts.

The Galatians offered sacrifices to appease their idols and gods, yet lived in constant superstition and fear. It was to these people that Paul, in one of his missionary journeys, preached the liberating power of Christ. They accepted this power and freedom and their lives were changed!

It could be that you need to be set free from the withering effects of self-criticism or from what seems to be a dull existence. Maybe you need to be lifted from religious legalism or from some other human control that is robbing you of freedom and stifling your personality. The message we attempt to communicate via NIGHTSOUNDS is that Christ frees us from bondage. He meets us at the point of our most profound need.

It could be that it seems to you that He is taking more time to accomplish this than you would like Him, but His timetable is right for each of us. What we need to do is to abandon ourselves to the flow of His liberating power, then allow Him to take care of the pace.

On a recent album we recorded a song that says: "He makes all things beautiful in His time." Let's remember that concept -- that we don't have to accept a dull or difficult situation to find meaning. The test of freedom from fear, sin, passion, meaninglessness -- or whatever fetters you -- may even be at the point of staying in the same situation, yet finding in it something other than we have known before.

You are loved, accepted by God, and are free to live life, not under the judgment of others, but responsible only to Jesus Christ Himself!

> "For dear brothers, you have been given freedom: not freedom to do wrong, but freedom to love and serve each other."
> (Galatians 5:13 LB)

THROW AWAY SOCIETY

There are two types of people in this world: those who throw beer cans alongside the road and those who pick them up.

I suppose there are some people who truly believe that we live in a "throw-away society" that permits us to toss everything away.

But what happens when there is no more "away"? We are told, that as good citizens we should be concerned about the environmental impact and consequences of such thoughtless acts.

It's shocking that it's taken us this long to wake up to the ecological mess modern mankind has created. What were we thinking about two or three decades ago?

Maybe we missed the point. God gave us dominion of this lovely planet and its delicate environment. Dominion. Not domination. We apparently got off in the wrong foot when God said "subdue the earth" and we took it as domination. But that's not what God's Word implies at all. We've wanted to "control" and "conquer" the cosmos for so long, maybe we thought we could do that with natural resources as well.

We've never been given a license to plunder and waste. But we <u>have</u> been given a sacred trust. And as stewards, we had better start valuing -- and exercising -- our dominion, don't you think?

> "And thou shalt do that which is right and good in the sight of the Lord: that it may be well with thee..."   (Deuteronomy 6:18)

KINDER AND GENTLER

Do you know that the country of Costa Rica has no army? It really doesn't have much of a police force either.

And yet, Costa Rica exists surrounded by the most war-torn countries of Central America: El Salvador, Nicaragua, and Panama.

Costa Rica is a democratic nation, with a good economy, and a stable government.

It has been an exporter of peace for many years; it has never had a serious quarrel or confrontation with a neighbor. It's never even taken sides or antagonized another country in even a small way. Truly, Costa Rica is a "kinder, gentler, nation."

As individuals, we can learn a lot from this little country. When we aren't out to attack, we find we don't have to shore up our defenses.

There is a great deal of cost and energy expended on attacking or defending.

Not all power comes from a gun. There is a Gentler Power that knows a better way.

Jesus expressed it in the form of the Golden Rule, of the meek ones inheriting the earth. And even Solomon knew of this better way thousands of years ago:

"A soft answer turneth away wrath:
but grievous words stir up anger."
(Proverbs 15:1)

FORGIVENESS

When my son Randy was a little boy of eight, he came up behind me in the kitchen and, out of the clear blue sky, said something that could make the difference in anyone's day.

His words were so simple and uncontrived that I asked him later to write it down so I could share it with you. So, he did:

Today I asked God to forgive your sins and my sins. Now we are clean. Wasn't that good?

That's not only good … it's fantastic! It means we have been forgiven. But are we ready to "forgive others as we have been forgiven?"

George Herbert once wrote, "He who cannot forgive others breaks the bridge over which he himself must pass if he would ever reach heaven; for everyone has need to be forgiven." The person who receives and accepts the forgiveness of God must be forgiving of others.

If that is true, (and Jesus said that it is), then forgiving and being forgiven forms a crucial, central, and eternal factor for every life.

This is one of the reasons I begin almost every concert with these words, "I am here tonight because I have been forgiven. Lord, I have experienced your love. Let me share it here with others." What a beautiful launching platform to areas of personal outreach, the full extent of which can be known only to God!

> "But I say unto you, love your enemies, bless them that curse you, do good to them that hate you, and pray for them that despitefully use you, and persecute you."
> "And when ye stand praying, forgive, if ye have aught against any: that your Father also which is in heaven may forgive you ..."
> (Mark 11:25)

JUST SAY NO!

Kids, maybe even more than adults, feel the need to "fit in" -- to try to not be too different from the rest of their crowd. So they say, "Yes" a lot to peer pressure.

But today's teen faces a landslide of temptation that previous generations never knew. They, and we, live in an era of crack cocaine, AIDS, occult games, condoms in school, and countless other threats to their moral well-being than the dangers faced by their parents or grandparents a generation or so ago. So it's even more important to learn how to say no.

Today, experts tell us that teens are more likely to try escapism with sex, drugs, or even suicide. One girl who attempted suicide said, "It's not that I wanted to die, I just wanted the pain to stop."

Kids today find it harder to say, "No" because they lack meaningful, intimate relationships with adults who love them. My advice to them: reach out for your parents and, more importantly, reach out for a personal relationship with a living and loving God.

God will provide you with the self-esteem and self-confidence to "just say, no!"

"My son, if sinners entice thee, consent thou not."(Proverbs 1:10)

SPIRITUAL ANESTHESIA

The noise of millions of American automobiles. The chaotic "babble" of a hundred million television sets. And the quiet blur of millions of computer games ... all part of a frenetic pursuit of the "good life".

And while millions seek diversion by travel, TV, movies and games, countless others are caught in the fast lane of chemical dependence. Alcohol and drug use are at epidemic proportions.

One might think that our entire nation has been lulled into a hypnotic state -- sort of a cosmic coma. As these accelerated technologies saturate our lives, we've overloaded on activity if not knowledge.

But despite all we <u>know</u>, are we any closer to the Truth? Maybe we're living in a age of what I call Spiritual Anesthesia ... an existential fog.

Well, don't surrender to a <u>robotic</u> existence. It's time, instead, to once again become conscious! Take action. Shake off that hypnotic blur, that tranquilizing technological haze that surrounds you!

And take back what is yours, the true life and energy of a spirit being.

"I urge you therefore, brethren, by

the mercies of God, to present your bodies a living and holy sacrifice, acceptable to God, which is your spiritual service of worship.

And do not be conformed to this world, but be transformed by the renewing of your mind, that you may prove what the will of God is, that which is good and acceptable and perfect."(Romans 12:1,2 NAS)

DREAMING

Where does our future come from? From our dreamers! Yes, that much-maligned group holds the key to what we will become as a society. The label "dreamer" carries both positive and negative baggage. To our credit, everything great that has ever come into man's experience has come through the minds of our dreamers, our visionaries. Michelangelo, Da Vinci, Galileo, Columbus, Edison, Ford, and Moody were dreamers.

Oh yes, we'd never get there without the doers, the builders. These are the men who take the blueprints given them by the dreamers and create great monuments to man's vision and ingenuity.

Winston Churchill, himself a dreamer as well as doer, said, "We are so often mocked by the failure of our hopes." He knew that without those hopes, dreams and visions -- those that come at night, or by day -- there would never be blueprints for our tomorrows.

So go ahead and daydream ... just make sure to put foundations under your castles-in-the-air.

> "And it shall come to pass afterward, that I will pour out my spirit upon all flesh; and your sons and your daughters shall prophesy, your old men shall dream dreams, your young men shall see visions."
>
> (Joel 2:28)

> "Trust in the Lord, and do good; so shall thou dwell in the land, and verily thou shalt be fed. Delight thyself also in the Lord; and He shall give thee the desires of thine heart. Commit thy way unto the Lord; trust also in Him; and He shall bring it to pass."
>
> (Psalms 37:3-5)

TAKE UP YOUR CROSS

"Oh, it's my cross to bear."

I'm sure you've heard a friend, relative, or maybe even your favorite in-law say this. And sometimes it is a mockery, because the person's "cross" is self-inflicted ... and the individual is parading a false martyrhood. Or, perhaps the cross they bore was the small 14 karat gold one on a chain around their neck. That great symbol of sacrifice and shame was no more than a lucky charm.

But, that's not to say we don't carry crosses -- we do have burdens in our lives. But, we really don't carry them very well on our own. Even recovering alcoholics and drug addicts discover that they can't rid themselves of the cross they carry -- the "monkey on their back" -- without relying on a Higher Power, one greater than themselves. The "Higher Power" refers to a step of their self-help program. We know that Power more personally as the Lord God.

Still, we do have burdens. And our cross can be heavy. But our load can be lightened. Seek the strength of the One who said, "Give me your burden ... cast your care upon Me." His strength is made perfect in our weakness.

"But God forbid that I should
glory, save in the cross of our Lord

Jesus Christ ..." (Galatians 6:14)

"For the word of the cross is
to those who are perishing
foolishness, but to us who are being
saved, it is the power of God."
(Romans 1:18 NAS)

ARE YOU NORMAL?

Are you normal? According to Webster,
"normal" is "conforming to an accepted model or
pattern." We often lament the fact that our
children are pressured by their peers to do things
that will make them like their friends. But
maybe we adults are just as guilty. We are
cautious about stepping away from the status quo
or being thought of as radical in our faith or
beliefs.

Some people fear <u>not</u> being normal. It's
been that way all through history. No one wants
to "rock the boat." Yet, has any great event,
discovery, or movement ever occurred through
simple "normal" behavior?

Moses, the Apostle Paul, Luther,
Jefferson, and Lincoln were all considered a bit
"flaky" in their day. What if they had adopted

"an accepted model or pattern" of behavior or action for themselves?

The model, or the pattern, of anyone who considers himself or herself to be Christian ... was certainly not considered normal in Jesus' day. Nor would it be today.

To be balanced and tempered ... yes. But to conform? No.

Perhaps we aspire to a grand spiritual normalcy, that allows for diversity within unity ... to be different ... to be ourselves.

The Apostle Paul said we should not let the world squeeze us into its way of thinking, but to be transformed in our thinking by God's Spirit. (Romans 12:1,2)

"Normal" is normal when the conformity is to the pattern or model of the Bible.

> "But continue thou in the
> things which thou hast learned and
> hast been assured of, knowing of
> whom thou hast learned them ..."
> (2 Timothy 3:14)

122

BONDING

Do you remember that song by Dionne Warwick, "I'll Never Fall in Love Again"? In it, the singer swears off men, citing all the pain, heartache, and "chains that bind you."

She goes on to sing of how glad she is to be out of the relationship, and offers a stern warning to others. Of course, by the end of the song we realize she'll "never fall in love again, at least 'till tomorrow."

What brings us back, in a relationship that has created hurt and heartache? Are we human beings masochistic or gluttons for punishment? Or, do we have an innate mechanism that fosters bonding despite the pain and problems? There seems to be a bonding that compels us to seek a oneness with another human.

Why is this? It almost seems to be programmed within us, doesn't it?

In the same vein, God calls us to "bond" with Him, to seek a oneness, an intimacy, a trust. And, He will wait. Because He also knows our failures.

"We love Him, because He first loved us." (1 John 4:19)

"If ye know these things, happy are ye if ye do them."
(John 13:17)

EMPTY PLACES IN THE HEART

I know of a man my age who retired not long ago and died not long after. Some commented at his death that they think he passed away from boredom and not being able to be useful.

I know of another man who still has a prestigious job, lots of responsibility, and it's made him a very wealthy individual. Yet, recently, he has been talking of "empty days"

"At the end of the day, I don't have the impression that I have invested myself," he complained.

He probably realizes that the Inner Man needs more than security, power, and excitement on the job. We are unique, and we are drawn to "contribute" to the race in a way that no one else can. And perhaps these qualities are never really attained. The Apostle Paul said, at the end of his life, that these were things of value he had not achieved or attained, but he still kept pursuing the goal.

Pity the man whose company benefits and job "perks" are so compelling that he resists the call to go somewhere else where his talents are really needed. Our soul, spirit, mind, and body must meet the challenges of our job, but more than this, they must fill that inner void as well. If not, then indeed, "empty days" shall fill our lives.

> "... I count all things to be loss in view of the surpassing value of knowing Christ Jesus my Lord..."
> (Philippians 3:8 NAS)

RESCUED FROM DESPAIR

NIGHTSOUNDS is an instrument of rescue, according to much of our listener response. This rescue may be from depression, insomnia, suicide, boredom, fear, even ... despair. A great number of people are fearfully uncertain about their future. Although the threat of nuclear war has lessened over the past few years, there are other ghosts on the horizon: ecological and natural disasters, economic collapse, AIDS; and the loss of moral values on an ever-growing scale.

Many are silent about these ghastly prospects and try to push them onto the back burner of their immediate thinking. Yet, studies, polls, and surveys confirm that the great majority of people are expecting some fearful catastrophe. Some people even get angry at God because they think He has abandoned them in the midst of these troubles. Others become fatalists.

And some act out their rage and despair on their world through violence.

Imagining the worst for yourself or those you love is self-inflicted torture.

We at NIGHTSOUNDS try encourage our listeners to remember:

-- that God loves the world and is in control.

-- that God is aware and is concerned about our immediate and long range personal problems and "is touched with the feeling of our infirmities."

-- that God offers us peace and confidence through faith in His Son, Jesus Christ.

If there is a single continuing message of NIGHTSOUNDS it is one of hope.

Please remember, you are not the only one living close to tears. Fear and despair are universal, even among Christians. But the despair we feel and which frightens us, can, through Christ, become the glue that holds us together. We talk about it on the air. We admit that we're vulnerable. We can hold up one another's burdens in prayer, "so fulfilling the law of Christ." What a responsibility and privilege to reach out in this way to a hurting world.

"We are pressed on every side by troubles, but not crushed and broken. We are perplexed because we don't know why things happen as they do, but we don't give up and quit. We are hunted down, but God never abandons us. We get knocked down, but we get up again, and keep going. That is why we never give up. Though our bodies are dying, our inner strength in the Lord is growing every day."

(2 Corinthians 4:8-9,16 LB)

THE LANGUAGE OF LOVE

Love can be forceful or as gentle as a whisper. It can be communicated directly in something as tangible as a fifteen page letter written on both sides of the paper ... or non-verbally through a gesture, or a facial expression ... the lingering glance of two lovers.

During the past 25 years -- through general moral permissiveness, advertising, movies and TV -- we have been witness to the word "love" having been twisted from its moorings ... mis-labelled, mis-used, mis-interpreted and, certainly, misunderstood.

Why is it that so many of us see ourselves imprisoned and isolated while surrounded by those who claim to know and love us? It is at this very crucial place that we need desperately to see ourselves -- our true selves -- as accepted and loved. Acceptance means we want someone who will love us when we are unlovely, not turn us away when we are wrong or have stumbled. We want, and need someone who will understand us when doing so is beyond human logic or understanding. But where is such acceptance, such love to be found?

We are each born with the deep need for acceptance, reassurance, and intimacy whether we realize it or not. You and I can ordinarily find this kind of love in our families and between friends. But too often such love is not there when we need it.

Yet, if our search for the fullest expression of love has been rejected or thwarted on the human level, we can be assured that in the person of Christ we can experience fulfillment in the three basic needs of humankind: someone to love, something to do, and something to look forward to.

Human love, although imperfect, can be blessed and enriched by the touch of God's divine, unconditional love, through the incarnation of Jesus Christ.

> "Dear friends, let us practice loving each other, for love comes from God and those who are loving and kind show that they are the children of God ... God showed how much He loved us by sending His only Son ..." (1 John 4:7,9 LB)

STRANGE FRIENDS

They say you can tell a man by the company he keeps. Maybe it is easier to read a person's character if he hangs out with his friends in a tavern, drinking and swearing. It would be difficult <u>not</u> to put someone into the same category of character of behavior based solely on appearances.

Maybe those of you who were kids in the sixties or seventies know what I'm talking about. Your companions wore long hair, torn bell-bottom jeans and scruffy tie-dyed shirts, and were accused of having no respect for cleanliness, grooming or good appearance.

"But what will people <u>think</u> if they see you with them?" was a popular parental refrain.

Maybe things haven't changed all that much and some of you young people can identify with that even today as you are judged by the friends that <u>you</u> keep.

Well, you didn't turn out so bad -- so maybe you <u>can't</u> judge a person by the company he keeps. That was certainly the case two thousand years ago, when twelve men, a rag-tag team of dissimilar individuals, were brought together to befriend a Man who called them to carry a message. Even the Man, Jesus, was criticized for his associations -- accused of being with drunkards, prostitutes and a whole assortment of sinners and unsavory types.

Strange friends? Even then, they were judged by appearances. Yet, appearances can sometimes be deceiving.

> "And when the Pharisees saw this, they said to His disciples, 'Why does your Teacher eat with the tax-gathers and sinners?' But when He heard this, He said, 'It is not those who are healthy who need a physician, but those who are ill ... for I did not come to call the righteous, but sinners.'"
>
> (Matthew 9:11-13 NAS)

SLOW DOWN

Nikos Karzenzakis in his book, Zorba the Greek comments on the "hurry sickness" of the 20th Century.

He writes: "One morning, I discovered a cocoon just as the butterfly was making a hole in its case preparing to come out. I was impatient so I breathed on the cocoon to warm it, to prompt his appearance. A miracle began happening. The butterfly started crawling out. And I shall never forget my horror. Its wings were folded back. The warmth of my breath had brought it forth prematurely. It struggled to live, but then died in my palm."

It is often a great and terrible wrong to violate the laws of nature. We should not hurry. With all things, God has His own time.

It is interesting to see the contrasts of that idea in Scripture. In Psalm 70:1, David cries out to God: "Make haste, O God, to deliver me; make haste to help me, O Lord."

Yet, over and over throughout the Psalms, God seems to have a different sense of timing. His word is "be still ... " "fret not", "wait patiently."

Finally, David learned the lesson of trust. His experience with the Lord had taught him God's faithfulness and not to worry about hurrying up the process. We, too, can learn to have this confidence:

> "Even before there is a word on my tongue, behold, O Lord, Thou dost know it all."
>
> (Psalms 139:4 NAS)

> "On the day I called thou didst answer me ... and thy right hand will save me."
>
> (Psalms 138:3,7 NAS)

WISE COUNSELORS

Do you know someone who needs professional help for an emotional or psychological problem?

Years ago, if someone had to see a psychiatrist, psychologist or other mental health counselor, he would often be looked at as some kind of person to be pitied or avoided, as though somehow his or her emotional problem were contagious.

That's changing now, and it's a welcome sign, for we <u>all</u> need counselling now and then. We all have problems that call for the professional assistance of others.

Even lawyers know this. Though they serve as counselor to their client, if <u>they</u> personally ever need legal help, they always seek a colleague's advice ... unless, as the old saying goes, he is a fool.

Wise counsellors are the first to acknowledge that they also need advice. It is the wise person who listens.

> "Where no counsel is, the people fall ..." (Proverbs 11:14)
> " ... and His name shall be wonderful, Counsellor, the mighty God, the everlasting Father, the Prince of Peace." (Isaiah 9:6)

COPING IN THE VALLEY

It's great to be at the zenith, the mountaintop.

But what of the valleys? You know the feeling. You're going through an experience of difficult personal stress or spiritual confrontation and someone asks, "How're you doing?"

And you reply, "Great!" But in truth, things aren't really so great.

We all have our confrontations in our personal valleys. We can't always be on an emotional or spiritual high. We'd probably burn out. Sometimes we're given an insightful vision in life, and yes, it does pump us up. It exhilarates us, as it should

But then comes the time for assimilating it. We face the test of what we've been shown on the mountaintop. It must be put into daily practice in the valleys. And this tedious, day-to-day application seems a long way off from the mountaintop days of insight, inspiration and exhilaration.

No, there's nothing like the breathtaking view from the mountaintop, but the real growth takes place in the valley.

> "Yea, though I walk through
> the valley ... thou art with me ..."
> (Psalms 23:4)

OBSESSIVE ... COMPULSIVE

What drives you? After you achieve a success plateau, do you sometimes still feel unsatisfied with yourself? People congratulate you for your achievement, but you don't think it was such a "big deal." And that long-awaited promotion? You wonder if you even deserve it. We all too often base our self-worth and sense of who we are on what we have done, or haven't done.

We live in a nation where obsessive-compulsive behavior may be "the norm."

But where in our Christian world view or theology did we learn that our self-worth is based on our accomplishments?

Or that activities which have no apparent goal are a waste of time?

Maybe as children we were praised for what we did rather than who we were. This has certainly been the case in my growing up years, and yours, too, if you think about it.

Pleasing people became our goal. We had to do this or that -- make this achievement or goal, break that record, then, we could parade our list of accomplishments before others and prove that we were "somebody". Or lament our failure to make such achievements.

But God doesn't think this way. His Word says, "Don't think too highly" -- or too

<u>lowly</u> for that matter -- "of yourself." Sober judgment is a virtue. You are loved, not by what you do ... but because of who you are. We must not forget that.

> "... what doth the Lord thy
> God require of thee, but to fear the
> Lord they God, to walk in all His
> ways, and to love Him, and to serve
> the Lord thy God with all thy heart
> and with all thy soul ..."
> (Deuteronomy 10:12)

ALONE ... IN THE CROWD

There I was, on an airport bus after a long and tiring business trip to the West coast.

I remember feeling somewhat depressed, as though I had failed at a certain endeavor. And suddenly, like a great crashing wave overwhelming me, I felt alone, humiliated, a failure.

All the problems of my trip began to get the best of me, along with fatigue, and the fact I had no one on the bus with whom I could share my hurt and frustration.

I began to look around. How many on the bus were like me: alone in the crowd?

I could have mentally "changed the subject" and blocked out the loneliness. But I didn't. Sometimes we wallow in our loneliness and it leads to self-pity. But other times, it may serve a useful purpose to allow the feelings to come through, to face them.

In doing so, you have a choice ... to live as a victim of loneliness ... or to see life as a gift, and accept it.

The solitary life need not be a lonely one. There is One who comforts the lonely as one who stays by that person, who "sticketh closer than a brother." There were times in His own life that Jesus was alone, His disciples and friends either could not or would not stay with Him. So He fully understands the feelings of the person who is alone even in a crowd, and understands the cry of that person's heart.

> "Turn to me and be gracious to me, for I am lonely and afflicted. The troubles of my heart are enlarged; bring me out of my affliction and my trouble, and forgive all my sins."
> (Psalms 25:16-18 NAS)

SPEAK UP!

Haven't you ever heard someone say,"Oh, my wife doesn't understand me," or "My husband doesn't communicate with me"? It seems that quite a few marriages limp along because of a "lack of communication."

But maybe that's a misnomer.

You see, with eye contact, body language, even silence ... we're always communicating something. It's not a <u>lack</u> of communications, then, but the <u>kind</u> of communications we're doing.

Problems crop up in relationships when we stop sending -- and listening to -- messages of love, care, and concern. One party believes she's a victim ... another shouts to get his way. No wonder that messages become garbled ... and even get lost in the process.

So, make sure that you're sending the right signal. Do your actions and body language confirm your communications and reinforce your original pledge, "I love you"?

And, if your messages aren't congruent, try the highest form of communication -- <u>prayer</u>. Prayer is the act of not only <u>sending</u> messages, but of receiving them as well.

"The Lord is nigh unto all
them that call upon Him, to all that

call upon Him in truth.

(Psalms 145:18)

"Confess your faults one to another, and pray for one another ... the effectual fervent prayer of a righteous man availeth much."

(James 5:16)

FINALLY ... HOME

Benjamin Franklin once compared the experience of dying to that of entering this world as a baby.

A baby is in its mother's womb, snug and warm. It's safe and nourished and has need of nothing. Its world is secure, and known. When it's time to be born, the baby demonstrates that it obviously doesn't care too much for the idea.

It's forced out into a new world of glaring light, strange and fearful loud noises, and even stranger big creatures. The baby resists having to come into this new life and world. It fights and wails, unhappy and afraid at being torn from the safe and comfortable world it knew. Yet, a few minutes after the birth, in its mother's arms, the baby realizes, "This is not too bad after all."

Just as our initial birth opened up to vast experiences, so will the culmination of our experience called our second birth. It's this second birth that opens us to an even more exhilarating existence.

So death, is simply "birth" into the Real Life and eternity. And in God's arms, we will say, "This isn't bad after all!"

"O death, where is thy sting?
O grave, where is thy victory?"
                    (1 Corinthians 15:55)

"And God shall wipe away
tears from their eyes; and there shall
be no more death, neither sorrow,
nor crying, neither shall there be
any more pain: for the former
things are passed away.
                    (Revelation 21:4)

LOVE REVIVED

A man started married life with a heart full of emotions and of a consuming love for his wife.

But as time passed, business took more of his attention, and thoughts of his wife were pushed farther back in his mind

Eventually the relationship grew stale. And finally, all traces of that original love seemed gone.

Can you revive love? The statistics seem to tell us that it is not possible to revive the feelings of love a person once had for his or her spouse. Divorce rates, even in our churches, have skyrocketed. There seems to be an epidemic of lost love.

So, is it really possible to revive love? Yes! But only if you tap into a Higher Source ... a Higher Love.

This type of Love can revive a lesser one.

That is ... you might try expressing love, not because you feel love for that person at that moment. But if you act in the conscious effort of allowing a Higher Love to express love to that person through you, you'll be amazed at what happens.

Love can actually be revived! but it happens only when you draw from the source of Perfect Love. True love began as an act of the will. To revive love, the action is the same.

> "... love one another; as I have loved you, that ye also love one another ..."   (John 13:34)

> "Be kindly affectioned one to another ... in honor preferring one another ..."   (Romans 12:10)

> "... let us not love in word ... but in deed and in truth."
> (1 John 3:18)

CIRCUMSTANCES AND GOD'S GUIDANCE

I'm very thankful that I have more than circumstances to guide me. When believers are guided only by events around them, and react to circumstances alone, they can get themselves into all kinds of trouble. But when we add prayer and a knowledge of the Scriptures to what is happening to us, we will have evidence of God's guidance.

This was pointed out to me a few months after launching the NIGHTSOUNDS ministry. At a critical moment in our operation, we were reminded of God's promise to lead, and we prayed for specific assistance. Within a few hours circumstances confirmed that we were to "proceed on course!"

But if we had relied only on circumstances, a different decision and direction might have resulted. Circumstances should not be followed if they contradict God's Word or seem opposite of what you glean from prayers.

As someone has said, prayer, Bible study, and circumstances are like three sets of lights used to guide an airplane onto the landing strip. The plane must come in on the point where all three lights line up. Just as any experienced pilot would not rely only on one lighted path, being guided only by circumstances alone is not safe.

Let me illumine three scriptural "paths" to guide you rightly -- ones that have made and will make the difference.

1.   "Whatsoever ye do, do it heartily, as to the Lord, and not unto men, knowing that of the Lord ye shall receive the reward of the inheritance: for ye serve the Lord Christ".   (Colossians 3:23-24)

2.   "God is able to make all grace abound toward you; that you, always having all sufficiency in all things, may abound to every good work".   (2 Corinthians 9:8)

3.   "He said unto me, 'My grace is sufficient for you: for my strength is made perfect in weakness'".
                    (2 Corinthians 12:9)

ABUSE OF POWER

"You're a slob! Clean up your room!"

"Don't be so stupid! Can't you ever do anything right?"

These are abusive words and it's sad to see how often they are tossed at children. Kids listen to what their parents tell them. And they believe it.

On TV last night, a documentary program spoke to the awful truth of child abuse. The sins of sexual child abuse and physical abuse of children are terrible things. But the program told of another kind of abuse, less violent but every bit as emotionally crippling as the other forms of child abuse.

Parents sometimes misuse their power as adults and verbally abuse their children with devastating emotional or psychological results.

Perhaps you've run out of patience, or you've had a bad day, or maybe you think, "I got to put a fire under this kid."

The truth is we'll never motivate a kid by calling him stupid. We might, however, break his spirit and forever cripple his sense of self-worth.

Parents need to be reminded that words can hit as hard as a fist. Take time to listen to what you're saying. You might not believe your ears.

"'There will always be temptations to sin', Jesus said one day to His disciples, 'but woe to the man who does the tempting. If he were thrown into the sea with a huge rock tied to his neck, he would be far better off than facing the punishment in store for those who harm these little children's souls. I am warning you!'"

(Luke 17:1-3 LB)

INVISIBLE SERVANT

A friend and colleague in the ministry, Dr. Richard Halverson, is one of these rare individuals who has been a constant source of personal inspiration to me. I recall when he was elected Chaplain of the U.S. Senate.

Dr. Halverson sought the counsel of friends and the prayers of his family as he considered taking this prestigious position. His family understood his initial reluctance to accept this role, but it soon became apparent that God wanted him to accept Senator Mark Hatfield's offer of the nomination. He formally was elected and sworn in on February 2, 1981.

He asked his fellow Christians, "Pray that I'll stay invisible and not use this prestigious position for personal gain or as a platform to address the nation."

This is good counsel to all of us who represent Christ in these momentous days. Even in the midst of our own public visibility or more private, personal ministry, may we hold up Jesus Christ: not using our position as Christian servants for private gain or advantage.

> "Blessed is the man that walketh not in the counsel of the ungodly, nor standeth in the way of sinners, nor sitteth in the seat of the scornful. But his delight is in the law of the Lord; and in His law doth he meditate day and night. And he shall be like a tree planted by the rivers of water ... and whatsoever he doeth shall prosper."
> (Psalms 1:1-3)

SUPPERTIME

It's a scene from a Norman Rockwell painting right out of the Forties or Fifties. You get the picture: Dad, Mom, and the kids are all sitting around the dinner table. There's obvious joy as together they eat supper and share their days' stories.

We don't see that very much anymore -- but there used to be a time when people weren't always in a hurry, gulping down their food in shifts -- kids microwaving a pizza to eat while they do homework or watch TV.

Mom snacks on leftovers before heading to the mall before they close. Dad, tired after his bout with rush hour traffic, pops his own microwave meal into the oven as he watches the news on TV.

Things sure have changed since that Norman Rockwell style suppertime.

Back then, suppertime was a time for more than just physical nourishment. It was a break from the rigors and stresses of life. It was time of family interaction, communication, learning ... a time of spiritual and emotional sustenance.

So the next time you find yourself racing about, grabbing for some fast food on the way to your next appointment, you may want to stop and ask yourself if you aren't missing something.

And you may wish to pledge to make your suppertimes more spiritually and mentally nourishing.

After all, man does not live by bread alone.

> "Thou wilt show me the path
> of life: in thy presence if fullness
> of joy; at thy right hand there are
> pleasures for evermore.
>
> (Psalms 16:11)

HEALING THE HEALERS

Do you ever wonder who counsels the counsellors? Who analyzes the psychoanalysts? Who treats the therapists?

A common misconception is that those who work at anything that might be described as therapeutic -- be it physical, emotional, or spiritual -- have "got it all together." That's not true. We all need someone to lean on. Wise counsel comes in every shape and form, and not always from clinical and professional sources.

I'm reminded of a story about a famous actor and an old preacher. Coincidentally, each was invited to recite the 23rd Psalm before a large crowd. The actor went first. His stage presence was commanding and his gestures had been perfected to poetic movements. He raised and lowered his voice dramatically to give every emotional nuance of the passage. When he concluded, the audience burst out in thunderous applause.

When the old preacher came up to the stage, he carried a worn Bible and held it to his chest. Silently he looked to heaven and began in a slow hushed voice. He had no apparent eloquence but had gone only a few words into the familiar passage when the crowd became quiet, and faces in the audience began to show an intensity and sincerity never before seen. Before the minister finished, there was hardly a dry eye in the audience and it was several moments before anyone could speak.

Finally, it was the actor who approached the minister, and grasped his hand. "My friend," he said with a smile, "what happened here is apparent. I know the Psalm ... but _you_ know the Shepherd!"

> "The steps of a good man are ordered by the Lord: and he delighteth in His way. Though he fall, he shall not be utterly cast down: for the Lord upholdeth him with His hand." (Psalms 37:23-24)

PERHAPS TONIGHT!

"As the twigs of a tree become tender ... you know that summer is near." Jesus used this analogy of a budding tree to point to a different kind of changing season.

Look all around you.

Never before in the history of the human race has there been a culmination of such amazing scientific cultural and world developments as there are now. The Iron Curtain has rusted ... the Berlin Wall has fallen ... weather patterns are strangely erratic ... and the world, brought together by mass communication, has become a singular, global village. And the former threat of nuclear annihilation has given way to countless civil wars and the actions of tyrants and would-be dictators.

The twin observations of Scripture about times such as these is both convincing and seemingly contradictory: (1) the world is getting better, and (2) the world is getting worse. But it is possible they are both sensible interpretations of current events. The first is a promise for the "last days": "I will pour out My Spirit on all mankind." This is the promise of better things.

The second prophecy reminds us that " ... in the last days perilous times shall come," and this is the promise of worse days before us.

We stand at the end of the 20th century in

stunned silence ... and sense we are at the threshold of new history -- we sense a Second Coming.

The scientists and the so-called "culteral elite" among the masses may laugh; but they also laughed at Noah.

Even so, be reminded as Jesus warned, when you see all these things, you know it is near, right at the door.

" ... in the last days it is going to be very difficult to be a Christian. For people will love only themselves and their money; they will be proud and boastful, sneering at God, disobedient to their parents, ungrateful to them, and thoroughly bad. They will be hardheaded ... constant liars and troublemakers and will think nothing of immorality. They will betray their friends ... Don't be taken in by people like that.
(2 Timothy 3:1-5 LB)

VENGEANCE

Not too long ago a man on the New York City subway system got fed up with muggers and thieves who roamed the subway cars looking for victims. This man took a gun with him and turned away robbers who threatened him, killing one in the process. Somehow, the act of killing an alleged criminal seemed to satisfy the masses who wanted justice. But others have suggested that perhaps he was seeking vengeance instead.

We agree that robbers and muggers should be held accountable.

But should the <u>killers</u> of robbers also be held responsible? Yes. Every man must be responsible for his acts.

And shall even the robbers be forgiven? -- or only the vigilante?

Well, some would say that's another story.

When we stop to consider it seems we can't even answer our own serious questions of love and hurt, solve the basic riddles of aging and death ... we can't keep ourselves out of wars or even feed ourselves properly.

In short, we don't know what we're doing.

Perhaps it was the Lord Jesus Christ, who from the cross, best understood the confusion of love and hate through vengeance. He said,

"Forgive them, Father, for they know not what they do."

Maybe hitting evil over the head is not the best way to rid the world of it. I don't think God ever intended us to be either a willing victim or avenging vigilante. Perhaps there is room for "knowing" somewhere between the extremes.

" ... Vengeance belongeth unto Me, I will recompense, saith the Lord." (Hebrews 10:30)

"Be beautiful inside, in your hearts, with the lasting charm of a gentle and quiet spirit which is so precious to God." (1 Peter 3:4 LB)

FEAR OR FAITH?

What keeps you from getting that better job? And what stops you from going up to that pretty girl and asking her out? Why can't you go up to your boss and ask him about that raise?

No doubt the reason is the same in each situation. It's fear that keeps us from doing the things we really love to do.

Psychologists and theologians usually agree on very little. Yet, they both agree that fear is our most debilitating emotion. Fear chains us and immobilizes us with handcuffs of helplessness.

Fear keeps us from being who we truly are. And as a result of such an overpowering force, we walk under a cloud of fear, seeing nothing but evil all around us.

We are not promised a life without evil, concern, or challenges that frighten and render us helpless. But when we call on God, we discover something stronger, something greater than fear, greater than ourselves.

The secret is faith. Hebrews 11 gives us a brief history of those who overcome fear by faith. The two words seem to be opposite sides of the same coin.

Fear is a focus on the future with apprehension and unreasonable concern.

Faith is a focus on the future with

confidence and an expansive supply of resources and strength.

> "And He said unto the, 'Why are ye so fearful? how is it that ye have no faith?"   (Mark 4:40)

> "There shall no evil befall thee, neither shall any plague come nigh they dwelling. For He shall give His angels charge over thee, to keep thee in all thy ways."
>   (Psalms 91:10,11)

T-G-I-M

"T - G - I - M!"
"Thank God it's Monday!"
No doubt you've heard the variation of this saying -- the T.G.I.F. expression looking forward to a weekend for rest and relaxation. But I don't think you have heard "Thank God it's Monday!" around the workplace lately.

There are always plenty of people who are happy to see Friday come around ... but Monday? Going-back-to-work-Monday?

It's a pity that so many Americans see

their work only as a burden instead of a way to achieve satisfaction and great happiness. Typically our attitude is that work is mainly a place for accumulating wealth, not joy.

We believe the expression: "You can't make money at what you love ... and you can't love what makes you money." But that's a myth!

We are exhorted to do our work with all of our heart ... and surely the heart is the seat of not only joy ... but true feeling.

> "And the Lord thy God will make thee plenteous in every work of thine hand ..."
>
> (Deuteronomy 30:9)

> " ... every man should eat and drink and enjoy the good of all his labor, it is the gift of God."
>
> (Ecclesiastes 3:13)

ARE YOU CONTENT?

Recently, driving up to Michigan, I pulled into the right hand lane of the four lane highway and set my speed control at 55. It was a beautiful day, and I was content.

But suddenly I got a tongue-lashing from a fist-shaking passing driver who thought I was out of line for doing the speed limit! He was not content that I was doing 55 -- he wanted more.

Contentment ... it's not the "in" thing these days. We think that perhaps if we're content, we'll somehow lose prestige or we'll get lazy. We really believe that getting to the top is worth any sacrifice whatsoever. Our world is motivated by those who are not content. They want to go faster, higher, farther. They want more.

Be careful. You may end up worshipping at the shrine of discontent. Shakespeare, put it this way: "Striving to be better, oft we mar what's well."

If you must strive -- strive to welcome contentment into your life. This may be going against the grain, and it may be a process that may take some getting used to. But it's worthwhile -- and you, like the apostle Paul can say with genuine meaning:

"Let your moderation be

known to all men. The Lord is at hand. Be anxious for nothing, but in everything by prayer and supplication with thanksgiving let your requests be known unto God ... I have learned to be content in whatever circumstances I am ... I can do all things through Him who strengthens me."

(Phil. 4:5 KJV; 4:6,11,13 NAS)

PROFIT THROUGH LOSS

Have you lost something of value lately? How did you react?

In the Great Market Crash of October, 1929, many of those who lost the most, also lost all hope. Some of the greatest persons of that day chose leaping from skyscraper windows rather than face the future. Their names went from the business or society pages to the obituary column in a single day.

They could not see any profit they might have recovered after that loss. Their loss so enveloped their emotional focus and minds that it seemed futile to go on.

Many of us have been in that awful

situation where life and the future seemed utterly black and desperately hopeless.

Yet, sometimes, we have to "lose it all" before we gain insight and a reasonable perspective. And that's not just with money or other possessions ... some of us must lose a relationship, or a job, before we see that keeping it was not for our highest good.

Still, that's never easy to see or accept at the time of the loss. Yet God always provides something to fill the vacuum, that absence, which the person or thing left behind.

And usually, that replacement is a greater plus on the credit side of life's ledger.

> "But as it is written, 'Eye hath not seen, nor ear heard, neither have entered into the heart of man, the things which God hath prepared for them that love him.'"
> (1 Corinthians 2:9)

WHAT'S WRONG WITH ME?

Thomas Alva Edison, in his efforts to create the first incandescent light, was often chided for his "failures." After one ill-fated attempt, he responded to his critics: "I haven't failed. I've just discovered another way the lightbulb will not work."

To Thomas Edison, there were no failures in life -- just lessons to be learned.

Maybe you've worked and prayed hard for something, and still ... you've "come up short." Do you label yourself a "failure"? Do you cry out, "What's wrong with me?"

Or, do you see the outcome as simply another way or not reaching your goal? Maybe you've even learned valuable lessons along the way ... such as patience.

No, you haven't failed. There's nothing wrong with you. Take the results of falling short of the goal ... and let it send you in your renewed race toward the mark.

> "Fret not ... trust in the Lord,
> and do good ... Delight thyself also
> in the Lord; and He shall give thee
> the desires of thine heart. Commit
> thy way unto the Lord; trust also in
> Him; and He shall bring it to pass."
> (Psalms 37:1-5)

TIME MACHINE

What if we could take a time machine and go back in time?

Where would you go? Sometimes I think I'd like to witness the exciting inventive triumphs of DeVinci ... the explorations of Columbus ... or, perhaps experience first-hand the gallantry and courage of the various historical figures.

Even a look at the evil campaigns of a Caesar or Napoleon might be fascinating. And seeing Babe Ruth hit his sixtieth home run ... wouldn't that be something?

But most of all ... I'd like to go to the Holy Land some two thousand years ago ... and witness the events and words of the man from Galilee through the eyes and ears of those who were there.

Well, put on your crash helmet. Buckle yourself in. We're going for a little ride!

Not a ride of miles ... but one across space and time.

We'll set the time machine's clock to ... let's say about 30 A.D. Destination: the Middle East.

As real as life itself, we'll experience that time as now. The cloudless blue sky ... the hot, dry air, camels, wagons, crude houses.

And we'll talk to the people who lived there at that time. And they'll tell us, in their own words, the story of a special man, a holy man ... a humble man ... who performed miracles -- but not for His own power or glory.

Come. Will you join me on a special journey with my unique time machine? My time machine is the Bible in a contemporary version and an open mind. These will take me where I want to go.

> "For the word of God is living and active and sharper than any two-edged sword ..."
> (Hebrews 4:11 NAS)

> " ... the holy scriptures, which are able to make thee wise unto salvation through faith which is in Christ Jesus. All scripture is given by inspiration of God, and is profitable for doctrine, for reproof, for correction, for instruction in righteousness."(2 Timothy 3:15,16)

SPIRITUAL PERFUME

"You smell delightfully fragrant," said the gravel walk to the bed of chamomile flowers which bordered the path.

"It's because we have been walked upon," replied the flowers.

"Does that cause such fragrance?" asked the gravel walk, "Treading on me produces no wonderful smell of sweetness."

"Our natures are different," answered the chamomiles, "Gravel walks become only harder when they are being trodden upon. But there is an opposite effect on us. When we are pressed and bruised while the dew is upon us, we give forth that sweet smell you now delight in."

Someone sent me that anonymous little illustration and its subtle prose still rings of great allegory.

The message?

Trials come to the believer and non-believer alike. One curses the events and experiences ... and that person eventually becomes hardened and bitter. Another faces the same events and experiences but gains wisdom and offers a perfume of praise, grace and beauty that contributes to someone else's joy.

"But thanks be to God! For through what Christ has done, He

has triumphed over us so that now wherever we go He uses us to tell others about the Lord and to spread the Gospel like a sweet perfume. As far as God is concerned there is a sweet, wholesome fragrance in our lives. It is the fragrance of Christ within us, an aroma to both the saved and the unsaved all around us." (2 Corinthians 2:14-15 LB)

GOD'S SATELLITES

I live next to a state prairie preserve and often go for walks in the evening where it is quiet and where I can see into the darkness above to look at the stars or count the constellations.

I was staring up at this night sky recently ... and saw something man-made -- a satellite. What a reminder for the human race!

A satellite must first be boosted into space, with a great thrust of rocket power. Then with power and consistency of trajectory, the rocket's orbit moves higher.

Eventually the satellite separates from the second stage rocket in order for it to gain enough speed and centrifugal force to be completely free from the earth's gravity. At that point, the satellite has true freedom. No longer is it susceptible to tug of our planet, pulling it down to burn up in earth's atmosphere.

And, free from gravity, the satellite can travel endlessly and anywhere in space, with virtually no power consumption at all, so long as it is careful not to be attracted by the pull of some other large space object's gravity.

From our "launching" at birth we have two choices: to be pulled down into the lower, earthbound nature of sinful man -- and eventually consumed by the pull of a corrupt world -- or, to avoid this gravitational attraction and seek the unlimited freedom, beauty, and vision of the heavens.

> "But to as many as received Him, to them gave He power to become the sons of God ..."
>
> (John 1:12)

PERIPHERAL VISION

Ever wonder why someone like Joe Montana was such a great football player? Well, you can start by listing all the typical qualities: speed, strength, perseverance. But there's one quality that is often overlooked.

Joe Montana or any great quarterback has great peripheral vision, a sixth sense of what's happening around him. He has to see more than just his receiver downfield in his direct line of vision.

We can learn a lesson from Joe Montana. I'm not thinking so much as an athletic lesson, but as a metaphor in life.

Too often, we get caught up with just what's in front of us. We develop "tunnel vision." Of course we have to see our objective, where we're going. But healthy vision must also permit us to focus on what's going on around us. Not just the immediate mission, but also the periphery.

Maybe it's time for a "spiritual" peripheral vision test. Do you see those on the fringes who need you as much as those in your downfield line of vision?

If not, perhaps we need to develop a sixth sense to view those in our periphery in need.

"Since we have such a huge

crowd of men of faith watching us from the grandstands, let us strip off anything that slows us down or holds us back, and especially those sins that wrap themselves so tightly around our feet and trip us up; and let us run with patience the particular race that God has set before us." (Hebrews 12:1 LB)

HOW DO YOU ENDURE?

You've seen the poster, with the cat hanging onto the limb of a tree. The caption reads, "Hang on, Friday's coming!" It's a clever poster with a measure of truth. Too many of us lead "fingernail existences" too close to the edge. We get frazzled, snap at people -- even suffer from "burnout".

In his book "Before Burnout - Balanced Living for Busy People," Dr. Frank Minirth says studies show that people who consciously attempt to live in God's presence day-to-day do more than just hang on by their fingernails -- they endure.

Remaining strong and steadfast in our spiritual principles gives us roots and depth. We can endure. Witness the mighty oak tree whose genesis is an acorn -- "just a common nut, that held its ground."

> "Let us hold fast the profession of our faith without wavering; (for He is faithful that promised;) ... cast not away therefore your confidence ..."
> (Hebrews 10:23,35)

NOT ALONE

I remember one time when I played music for the often forgotten people at a local nursing home.

At the end of each song, the people sat, not showing much emotion. So I tried a different kind of song. Still no response. After several songs, I asked one of the attendants whether the people liked our music.

"Oh, he responded, "they like it very much, Mr. Pearce, but they are also saddened. You see, they think each song may be the last one you'll play for them ... and then you will go ... leaving them alone ... again."

It's not just the old and infirm who have

this sad sense of being left alone. We all have fear of being abandoned. And, since death is the greatest cause of loneliness, we have a certain kind of apprehension which tends to focus directly on this concern. Will my parent or spouse leave this earth before me? Might my child die first?

Remember Jesus' words, "I will never leave or forsake you." Let that promise fill you anytime you fear being left alone. With the truth of those words, it is not just comforting also a bit ironic that loneliness is not something we have to face alone.

> "For I am persuaded, that neither death, nor life, nor angels, nor principalities, nor powers, nor things present, nor things to come, nor heights, nor depth, nor any other creature, shall be able to separate us from the love of God, which is in Christ Jesus our Lord."
> (Romans 8:38,39)

> "I will not leave you comfortless: I will come to you ... Let not your heart be troubled, neither let it be afraid."
> (John 14: 18,27)

OH ... NO!

We've all had these experiences. Sometimes we even try and prepare for them so they will not be so devastating when they occur.

Maybe it's an engagement called off, or a business failure ... or when a child dies.

We whisper, "Oh ... no!" Amazing, isn't it, how much pain and despair can be packed into two small one syllable words?

An accident takes place and leaves one paralyzed. Or someone's house burns down. "Oh ... no!" A hurricane sweeps across an area and wreaks havoc, death and destruction. "Oh, no!"

Sometimes self-pity floods in when the "Oh no's" of life strike us. It's natural, I suppose, because we feel betrayed, hit from the blind side.

But it is at this very hour that difficulty or tragedy strikes that we must determine not to accept failure as our fate. Go back to your drawing board and refine your vision.

With God's help we can change our perspective, we can turn around the "Oh no's" of life. Often, the disillusionment, failure, or separation is preparing the way for God to bring the best into our life.

"The Holy Spirit helps us with

our daily problems and in our praying. For we don't even know what we shall pray for, nor how to pray as we should; but the Holy Spirit prays for us with such feelings that it cannot be expressed in words. And the Father who knows all hearts knows, of course, what the Spirit is saying as he pleads for us in harmony with God's own will. And we know that all that happens to us is working for our good if we love God and are fitting into His plans." (Romans 8:26-28 LB)

WAITING

"O.K., buddy ... move it or milk it! C'mon ... let's get this show on the road!" The sharp words were followed by a loud and long blast from the automobile horn behind.

You've heard those words on the highway before. May be <u>you've</u> even used them!

Often we experience varying degrees of frustration or distress when we have to wait.

But waiting doesn't have to be wasted time ... unless we allow it.

Patience has two aspects. <u>Active</u> <u>patience</u> is a perseverance that presses on with the business at hand. And, <u>passive</u> patience is an endurance that abides quietly and confidently under trial.

You can't hurry a chemical reaction the opening of a rose bud, the emergence of a butterfly from a cocoon, or the birth of a baby. So also, ideas, events or actions take their own time. And patience, in its way, brings a rich spiritual blessing.

> " ... is your life full of difficulties and temptations? Then be happy, for when the way is rough, your patience has a chance to grow. So let it grow, and don't try to squirm out of your problems.

For when your patience is finally in full bloom, then you will be ready for anything, strong in character, full and complete."

(James 1:2-4 LB)

THE FINISH LINE

One time I found myself in a mile race with champion runners. I got off to a great start. "Pretty good," I thought. Until I hit that last lap. Then while my legs weakened, the experienced track men pulled up from behind. One by one they ran right past me and I didn't even place!

That's the thing about races ... and just about anything in life ... it's the finish line that counts.

Persistence, of course, is the key. And, no matter how good you are, how far out in front you might think you are -- you've got to keep training. And you have to finish the race.

The Christian life is a life of faith, and it's an <u>active</u> lifestyle. You see, it's not the brightest or the most talented people who get the most out of life. Instead, the prize goes to those that are committed to a worthwhile goal for the entire race.

"In a race, everyone runs but only one person gets first prize. So run your race to win. To win the contest you must deny yourselves many things that would keep you from doing your best. An athlete goes to all this trouble just to win a blue ribbon or a silver cup, but we do it for a heavenly reward that never disappears. So I run straight to the goal with purpose in every step. I fight to win. I'm not shadow-boxing or playing around. Like an athlete, I punish my body, treating it roughly, training it to do what it should, not what it wants to do. Otherwise I fear that after enlisting others for the race, I myself might be declared unfit and ordered to stand aside."

(1 Corinthians 9:24-27 LB)

SIGNS

"Oh, Lord, just give me a sign!"

Have you ever prayed in that kind of direct way? Often we feel we must have a sign --- now. And not something subtle; no, we need some obvious sign, projected on the big screen. In sensurround stereo!

It's strange when you think about it. God has given us common sense, prudence, and intelligence. Our decision-making ought to be a fairly capable process with these qualities. And, the Lord has given us His Holy Spirit to provide inner guidance and direction. Still we look for a sign.

But such reliance on signs is usually a prescription for disaster. Signs suggest spiritual immaturity and they lead to superstition.

Yes, sometimes we do receive signs; yes, there are and have been miracles that serve as signs. But we must have an innocence about them.

Signs are gifts that come to us. They cannot be manufactured, and should not be sought.

    " ... The hand of our God is upon all them for good that seek Him; but His power and His wrath is against all them that forsake

Him. "   (Ezra 8:22)

"And ye shall seek me, and
find me, when ye shall search for
me with all hour heart."
                    (Jeremiah 29:13)

TOGETHER THEY STAND

If you've ever visited the great Sequoia
forests of the Northwest, you probably stood silently, gazing upward at the magnificent redwood
giants rising some 300 feet into the air from the
forest floor.

As one who has spent most of his adult
life in the Chicago area, a giant redwood tree is
an amazing miracle -- equivalent in size to a 30
story skyscraper!

But more amazing to me is the fact that
the forest rangers tell us that the giant redwoods
have a very shallow root system.   I'd   have
thought the roots from a sequoia tree would go
hundreds of feet into the earth. In truth, they are
so near the surface that any moderately strong
wind could topple the tree.

Except for one thing. The redwoods do
not grow by themselves. They all grow in

groves. Their roots spread out and intertwine with the roots of other redwoods, and the strength of these intertwining roots work to hold up all the trees. This interlocking root system makes it possible for the sequoia forest to withstand gale force storms and survive for centuries.

A sequoia by itself won't survive. It needs the support of others, and must give its support to maintain the lives of others.

I think this is a beautiful illustration of how God has designed His creation. And there's another beautiful parallel. He has designed us to need each other.

Our single roots are too shallow to keep us from being blown over by life's storms. But when our roots are intertwined with those of family, friends, our church and other believers, even the gale force winds of adversity can't dislodge us.

> "And he will be like a tree firmly planted ... The wicked are not so, but they are driven like chaff which the wind drives away."
> (Psalms 1:3,4 NAS)

WILLING TO FAIL

Before age 30, this man failed miserably in business -- <u>twice.</u> Then, he tried his hand at politics, but was defeated in a legislative race. Looking for stability in his life, he decided to get married. But before it happened, his sweetheart died. This was followed by a nervous breakdown.

Later, thinking he'd try politics again, he lost a congressional race. He was then 34, and two years later he lost another contest.

When he was 45, he lost a senate race. Two years after that he failed in his effort to become Vice President. And two years later, he lost another senatorial race. After spending all his adult life in attempts to achieve lofty, even noble goals, this man seemed to fail at everything he tried. His life seemed absolutely hopeless, and here he was at age 50 with failure dogging him at every turn.

Finally ... at age 52 ... he was elected President of the United States. The man's name was Abraham Lincoln.

Success is a seed born in the hearts and minds of men, and can flourish regardless of our past, regardless of so-called failures. James Russell Lowell rote, "Not failure, but low aim, is a crime."

An another thing to remember is that

"failure" is often a value judgement. Sometimes not getting something is God's way of protecting us from receiving less than His best, which we obtain when we wait upon Him. That's why it is okay to be willing to fail -- so long as it is not our faith and ultimate spiritual vitality that is affected by these setbacks.

> "And the Lord said ... I have prayed for thee, that thy faith fail not ..."   (Luke 22:31,32)

THE WORLD OF ME

Do you remember that famous astronomer who was nearly put to death in the Middle Ages? Galileo had the audacity to suggest that the earth revolved around the sun. Scientists, government, and even church leaders saw it the other way around! Puffed up with self-importance, they saw the earth -- not to mention themselves -- as the center of the universe. They could not conceive of a universe as being anything else.

We all know somebody who perceives himself as the center with the world revolving around <u>him</u> or <u>her.</u> It's no surprise that recent times were called the "Me Generation."

When we focus too intently on self we lose perspective, and the "order of things" becomes blurred. The grand spiritual irony is that man gains all the gifts of the kingdom -- not when he is consumed by self -- but when he <u>gives</u> of himself.

> "Then said Jesus unto His disciples, If any man will come after me, let him deny himself, and take up his cross and follow me. For whosoever will save his life shall lose it: and whosoever will lose his life for My sake shall find it. For what is a man profited, if he shall gain the whole world, and lose his own soul? or what shall a man give in exchange for his soul?"
> (Matthew 16:24-26)

> "For if a man think himself to be something, when he is nothing, he deceiveth himself."
> (Galatians 6:3)

EASTER

Suppose you flipped on the TV, turned to CNN, and heard this startling news. "There is this report out of the Middle East. A man in his early thirties, a teacher and spiritual leader, had been condemned to die. And, in fact, just days ago was put to death, yet today, amazing eyewitness accounts declare that He is now apparently alive!"

The TV report has your interest now. Someone was killed who is now alive?

The report continues, "As witnessed by hundreds of onlookers, the man was executed at 3:00 P.M. local time on Friday and on Sunday morning was seen walking and talking with friends, just as He had been doing days before. According to other accounts, this man had told his colleagues several days earlier that He actually would defy death. And, unbelievable as it seems, according to reports, He has done exactly that!"

Can you imagine the excitement and confusion that would have resulted if CNN and the other networks had covered the death and resurrection of our Lord?

Easter is God's reminder to us of all that He has done to redeem us and bring us to Himself. "Believest thou this?"

"He will swallow up death in victory ..."   (Isaiah 25:8)

"I am the resurrection and the life: he that believeth in me, though he were dead, yet shall he live: and whosoever believeth in me shall never die. Believest thou this?
(John 11:25-26)

MOTHER'S DAY

You know, Mother's Day is almost here. Sometimes, I think we take better care of our cars than our mothers. Maybe there should be a maintenance or service manual for mothers.

For example, mothers need a hot bath and nap every 100 miles. A baby sitter and night out every 1,000 miles. A one week vacation every 10,000 miles.

Her battery?   Recharge it regularly. Unexpected hugs and kisses ought do that nicely.

Brakes? See to it that she comes to a full stop occasionally.

Fuel? She survives on leftovers, but an occasional dinner for two at her favorite restaurant will add to her efficiency. That's dinner for two -- not the whole tribe.

No one more than mothers has any idea how much time it takes to love a child into maturity. Until they've had a child of their own, all the work is simply theoretical to those who have never been a mother. But cleaning up ... fixing meals ... soothing teething babies ... fixing formula ... driving to the pediatrician ... forever picking up ... changing diapers ... taking care of the bills ... it's all very real to these dedicated moms who wonder if they'll ever "get there."

Do you know that a mom who has cleaned up after three kids, by the time they reach eighteen, has put in more than 18,000 hours of additional housework -- work she would not have had to do if she hadn't had kids?

It makes us realize that all moms -- no matter where they are during the day -- are working moms.

> "Who can find a virtuous woman? for her price is far above rubies" (Proverbs 31:10)

> "She rises also while it is still night and gives food to her household ... her lamp does not go out at night ... she opens her mouth in wisdom, and the teaching of kindness is on her tongue. She looks well to the ways of her household ... her children rise up to bless her.(Proverbs 31:15,18,26-28 NAS)

FATHER'S DAY

Do you know who came up with the idea of "Father's Day"?

Well, it wasn't an egocentric male who figured he was due some respect.

Actually, it was a woman -- Mrs. J.B. Dodd -- who devised and prompted that special day over 65 year ago in Spokane, Washington. I suppose she felt that it would be a good thing, because moms already had their day set aside as a holiday.

So, we have a day set aside to honor both mothers and fathers. And that's appropiate. In this day of so much emphasis on traditional family values, it's a good thing to honor the two people who have done so much to shape our values and mold our lives.

So this day is to honor Dad. True ... sometimes he didn't do it right. But consider this: dads usually raise their kids the best way they know. Sometimes their role model may not have been the very best. But no one gives you a manual when you become a dad. So most of us just do our best and stumble along by "learning on the job"

So how about your father? Why not thank him in your heart -- and to his face if he is still alive -- for helping make your life what it is today.

And even if your father wasn't able to provide the best role model or dropped the ball as Dad, this is a good day to put all that aside and let love rule your heart.

> "Honor thy father ... that it may be well with thee, and thou mayest live long on the earth."
> (Ephesians 6:2,3)

THANKSGIVING

The day I started to write this, everything seemed to go wrong:
1. I ripped my good shirt.
2. I received an especially scathing letter from an atheist.
3. Two very stressful calls came from listeners.
4. I sprained my right shoulder lifting a heavy object.
5. I lost an important credit card.
6. Etc... Etc...

Since it was the day this devotional about "Thanksgiving" was due to the editor, I had to be careful to avoid a bit of cynicism. However, there are some verses of Scripture (besides Romans 8:28) that I've kept on the backburner for just this kind of test.

The first is Ephesians 5:20 "Always giving thanks to God the Father for everything in the name of our Lord Jesus Christ."

The clincher is 1 Thessalonians 5:18: "In everything give thanks ..."

So, at that point, I decided it was time for a little chat with myself:

"Okay, Pearce ... so you've had a few setbacks; have you thought about those who are really unfortunate? Do you pray for them? Aren't you grateful for a sound mind and body

... for the extensive ministry God has given?"

Like you, I need to be reminded from time to time that God is present with us through the entire spectrum of our lives. Although He allows the negative factors into our experience, it is for a purpose -- to deepen us and make us more like Himself.

Suffering is never fun ... but it's functional. It's purpose is not to embitter us ... but drive us to our knees.

Since God isn't finished with us yet, perhaps we can't honestly say with Job: "Though He slay me ... yet will I trust Him" (Job 13:15).

So, at this Thanksgiving season we all thank God for the obvious blessings. However, maybe after a few more pot holes, hard knocks, and detours down the road, we'll be able, with integrity, to say thanks for those as well.

> "Give thanks in all circumstances ... for this is God's will for you in Christ Jesus"
> (1 Thessalonians 5:18 NIV)

CHRISTMAS

A good many Christmases ago I purchased a toy stove for one of my daughters. She was about five years old at the time.

The first thing I saw inside the box was a rather large sheet of instructions for assembling this toy. I promptly put it aside because the assembly really looked fairly simple.

Yet, about a half-hour into this project, I began to feel uneasy.

The parts weren't fitting together properly. And the assembly began to look more difficult. Following a hunch, I unfolded the directions I had discarded earlier and saw 55 sequential steps to putting the toy stove together!

It wasn't until that moment that I saw that if I continued by my own design ideas, I was on my way to creating a disaster. So I had to take everything apart, and start all over -- this time deciding to go by the directions.

Why is it that so frequently the last resort in life if to read the directions?

Even in our day to day living we can make that application. It's best to follow the directions supplied by the Makers. We function best and are happiest when we follow the plans of our Creator. He knows what's best!